RECKLESS AT THE BORDER

सीमा पर लापरवाह

a dual memoir

Jane Parhiala

&

Pradeep Parashar

Publisher's Information

EBookBakery Books

Authors contact: Jane: parhialaindia@gmail.com
Pradeep: mariadeeptravel@gmail.com

ISBN 978-1-938517-94-5

Note from the authors: Because this is a memoir the events of this story are as true as our 70 year old memories allow. We have kept some of the real names and places with their permission. To protect our dear friends and those not so dear who wish not to be mentioned, we have changed their names. If we make up a name and it happens to be your name, please forgive us. It was not intentional. The currency throughout the book is in US dollars. It was easier not to deal with the exchange rate for each individual country.

Acknowledgments

When I started writing *Reckless at the Border* with Pradeep I had no idea how many people would be involved in the publication of this book. We thank our friends, strangers and relatives. I thank the members of the Cape Cod Writers Conference and the Pen Women of Cape Cod for their professional influence and support.

We give our thanks to:

Sandra Faxon, artist as well as wordsmith encouraged me from the very beginning with her knowledge of the English language and with her whimsical wit; the Beta Readers: Susan Heinlein, Kirk Stines, Chris Tarnay and Eleanor Neubert: I took their feedback seriously; my brother, Paul Parhiala; Jack Cook, Stephen Gordon, Emily Ferguson, Juanita Perez, Zachary Rothstein-Dowden, Perry Coppola, Dan Neelan and Kathryn Knight; the Record's Department at the Denver County Courthouse, Mataam Fez Restaurant in Denver, the Falmouth Public Library, and the University of Kentucky Libraries.

A special thanks to my husband Jim for being a patient listener who understood my need to travel to India to complete my dream; to my children, Kenneth and Kira who stayed enthusiastic even when my optimism was fading and a special thanks to Kira for the beautiful book cover.

And, of course, many thanks to the relentless and caring support of Michael Grossman of the EBook Bakery, my publisher, and to editor Jenna Bernstein. I am forever grateful to my editor Dan Robb, consultant, supporter, and dedicated interpreter of the written word.

And on the other side of the world in India, from Pradeep:

I want to thank each and every one who shared with

me all their experiences; to Jane Parhiala who typed and typed and typed long into the night; the general managers of the Rajasthan tourism hotels in Jaipur and Pushkar, for their comfortable rooms when we were touring while writing; to Siddharth Nandan for extra-long leave and for re-employing me as a general manager of Hotel Taj Plaza, Agra. Huge thanks to my family for their support: Usha Parashar, Priyanka, Anjali and my son Dr. Ashish Parashar for encouraging my itchy-travel feet.

All the vegetarian dishes: Palak paneer, Chana masala, Dal, Basmati rice and the variety of tasty breads in the world cannot express the gratitude I feel towards the general managers, M.S. Rana, and R.K. Rai, of M.P. Tourism hotels in Khajuraho and in Orccha.

A very special thanks to Earl Choldin for his nit-picking and constructive criticism.

Last, but certainly not least, I am very grateful to the friends who either played a starting role for this book or have been sounding boards during the process: Rakesh Kumar Chauhan, owner of the hotel, Pearl of Taj, Mahesh Parashar, Mahesh Kushwah, my sister, Kusum Parashar, brothers Anil, Rakesh and Dr. Sunil Parashar. Thank you for helping me tune in to my adventurous past! And thanks to:

Maps, by Stephen Gordon, pg. xxii, pg.100
Map, Jack Cook, pg. 120
Jane's photo, Emily Ferguson
Pradeep's photo, Arunkumar
Wedding photo, Malcolm Cook, 1979
Cover art and design, Kira Doutt
Cover layout, Blue Trimarchi
Interior & publishing, Ebook Bakery

For Jim, Kenneth and Kira

-J. P.

To mother, Yamuna and father, Hari

-P. P.

"It's not about how to achieve your dreams, it's about how to lead your life...if you lead your life the right way, the karma will take care of itself, the dreams will come to you."

Randy Pausch, *The Last Lecture*

Table of Contents

RECKLESS AT THE BORDER

How it all began

Agra, India, 2018, Jane

I stop to catch my breath as I climb the stairs to the fourth floor of the hotel. It would be less strenuous to stay in a room on the first floor, but I have been here before and enjoy the view from upstairs. My chai waits for me on the table at the rooftop restaurant. I sit and sip the hot spicy tea as I gaze upon the Taj Mahal, a sight I've learned to love. It stands in the distance, strong and majestic, to me, a white pearl etched with rich conflicting memories.

The caffeine and sugar from the tea makes its way to my brain and opens my tired eyes. It's been a long journey.

Cape Cod, Massachusetts, 2014, Jane

Papers, photos and letters were either piled high on shelves, stuffed in drawers or spread out on the floor. As I looked around at this mess, I realized the time had come to clean up and get organized. My daughter lived in Boston finishing her senior year at Massachusetts School of Art and Design and my son worked for the National Park Service in Northern California. Both children seemed content with their living situations and at least for the moment, were not living at home. My husband and I agreed to delve into the arduous task of sorting and throwing things out. We hated to admit it, but we both enjoyed squirreling away our little and sometimes not so little treasures.

I tackled the bedroom first and zoomed into the small wooden night table next to my bed. It had three drawers which were filled with writing paper, old cards and folders. I found myself looking for one folder in particular. I knew it was somewhere in one of those drawers, but which one? Then I found it.

The envelope, stained and crinkled with a little tear on the flap, sat in my hands, as if it were a fragile ancient scroll. Should I open it and be reminded of him once again? I paused, then slowly shook out its contents. My past came spilling out. There were still the questions: the whys, wheres and what ifs.

One by one the photos of all our dreams showed themselves: the smile on his face, the body I touched and kissed, the dear one who lied and deceived me (or did he?) The letters attempting to explain what happened.

I was not ready to dismiss the man from India whom I had married thirty-four years ago and had divorced. How could I? My wedding dress hung in my closet. I made it myself. The saris his sister gave me on our wedding day were neatly folded in a dresser drawer. (I could never figure out how to put them on!) A statue of Lord Krishna (the Hindu Deity of Love), which he left behind, sat on the window sill in the living room.

Giving myself permission, I slowly examined each picture, each letter pulling me into the past, feeling emotion and longing for answers, and somewhere deep inside, still a caring for him. After viewing the pictures through bleary eyes, I put the letters and photos back into the envelope, placed them ceremoniously in an unmarked box and carried it to the attic to be discovered by me again at a later date or by my children someday.

Meanwhile, convinced that I needed to keep up with my kids and society in this digital age, I reluctantly purchased a computer, and a techy friend set up a website for my weaving business. A week later, while I proudly admired my shiny new Mac and my web site, a submission appeared. So far, I had received only three, all from friends wishing me well, but on this particular day, the submission I received was from him, my former husband, Pradeep Parashar.

> September 8, 2014
>
> Hello Jane,
>
> So glad to see you doing
> well!
> After 34 years, I hope we can
> have some communication.
>
> It would be nice to hear from
> you, only if you wish.
>
> Best Regards
>
> With respect and love,
> Pradeep

I stared at the submission, reading each word over and over again; not believing that he had contacted me after all these years and just after I had discovered the envelope with all his letters and photos. I debated whether I should click "delete" or answer. I chose to respond:

September 11, 2014

My Dearest Pradeep,

How strange it is to type your name... 34 years! What a surprise! I hope you are well and life has given you joy. For me, the anger, the hurt and the deception has long passed. My dreams were shattered and I had to move on, as did you. The thing you can do for me now is to give me answers: the truth of what happened. Give me your story.

Jane

~

September 17, 2014

My Piece of Heart, hello Jane.

That's great to hear from you. It made my day. I am doing well, happy and healthy in India at present and trusting that you are happy and healthy as well. I know there are lots of things went untold. I would love to tell you each and everything which I have faced in this life; how painful time was in 1979-1980.

I would love to tell you the whole truth…please do not believe whatever they say about me because in fact, they really are far from the truth. Jane, you may have to ask me questions and I would love to reveal the whole truth as I understand. This was a very serious matter in our life's commitment. As to your question, What happened? I don't know where to start from. Please ask me in a way so that I can follow up on the specific questions. All I can truthfully say is that I didn't do anything wrong. Food and medicine were my top priority.

I hope you will continue this communication until the truth is discovered.

I am extremely happy to hear from you and trust that our communication after 34 years will be meaningful to you.

Please accept my kindest respect with love,

Forever,
Pradeep

~

After a few emails, we discovered that over the years we each had been telling "our story," each in our own countries, thousands of miles away, entertaining people at dinner parties, sharing our adventures with friends and even strangers over coffee or chai.

Words for this story have been floating in my head for thirty-four years and the introductory paragraph written over and over again. I wrote in journals, on scraps of paper and in little notepads only to be thrown out, scratched out or stuffed away in drawers. But I realized it could never be completed without his half of the story.

At some point during our "back and forth" emails, I suggested we write a book together. He suggested having someone else write it, but I thought it would be a fun project for us to do together.

Attempting to communicate our thoughts and ideas by email, however, turned out to be difficult. Wifi was not always working where Pradeep lived in India and he traveled often. The best thing to do was meet. With a mixture of trepidation, as well as great excitement, I flew to India.

As the plane landed in New Delhi, I asked myself, for the hundredth time, if this was the right thing to do. What was my real purpose? Would I show a hidden anger, or would I swoon and be vulnerable once again to his charms?

When I cleared customs, I escaped to the ladies' room, and examined myself in the mirror. My hair was a mess and gray. My face looked old and wrinkled. What did I expect at 67? We were in our early 30's when he last saw me and I had to remind myself that he too had aged. I shook off all these thoughts, took one last look at myself in the mirror, smiled, grabbed my bags and marched out to greet India once again.

Pradeep had said to walk through the glass doors to the outside and he would be there waiting for me.

"How will you know me?" I asked in the email "Oh, I'll know," he said

My heart was pounding. Would I recognize him? I needed not to worry. There he was walking toward me with his big smile, smartly dressed in a suit and tie. We stood there, staring at each other, speechless, pleased and amazed that we had arranged a meeting after all these years.

Now we have another dream. Let's see if we can make this one work.

Agra, India … 2014, Pradeep

There were few people on the street today, the heat was unbearable, and business was slow. I was operating an internet cafe called the 25 Hour Coffee Club. My partner, also with the last name of Parashar, and I decided to do some research on the Parashar family. While searching on Google, my ex-wife's image came in front of my eyes. I was so surprised that I burnt my mouth with my coffee. I clicked on a video where she was explaining her weavings which were displayed in an art gallery in Falmouth, Massachusetts. I was impressed. Without a second thought I sent a submission to her website, hoping she would respond.

In a few days I received an email from her. I answered and that was the start of our communication. After several months and many emails, we discussed the possibility of writing a book together. It was inevitable that we should meet, and she booked a flight to New Delhi.

I paced back and forth by the sliding doors of the Indira Gandhi International Airport, nearly out of cigarettes.

"She should be here any moment now," I thought, noticing my heart was beating a little faster than usual. When she came through the door, we both smiled. She looked like she did in the video so there was no problem recognizing her. Jane was my friend and had been my wife thirty-four years ago. This time I prepared to receive her as a guest. I led her to a waiting cab, and we were off to write our story

In 2015 Pradeep and I traveled through India by car, rickshaw and by train. It was on the train where he began to share the story of his life. He talked, I wrote. Over a span of five years we worked together writing down the events of his life. We worked on the manuscript in Orccha, Khajuraho, Pushkar, Pachmarhi and in Agra. I returned to Agra several times to listen, write and revise.

In Part One Pradeep tells the story of his long turbulent journey to the United States. I tell my story in Part Two and the book continues with our adventures together.

Namaste,
Jane

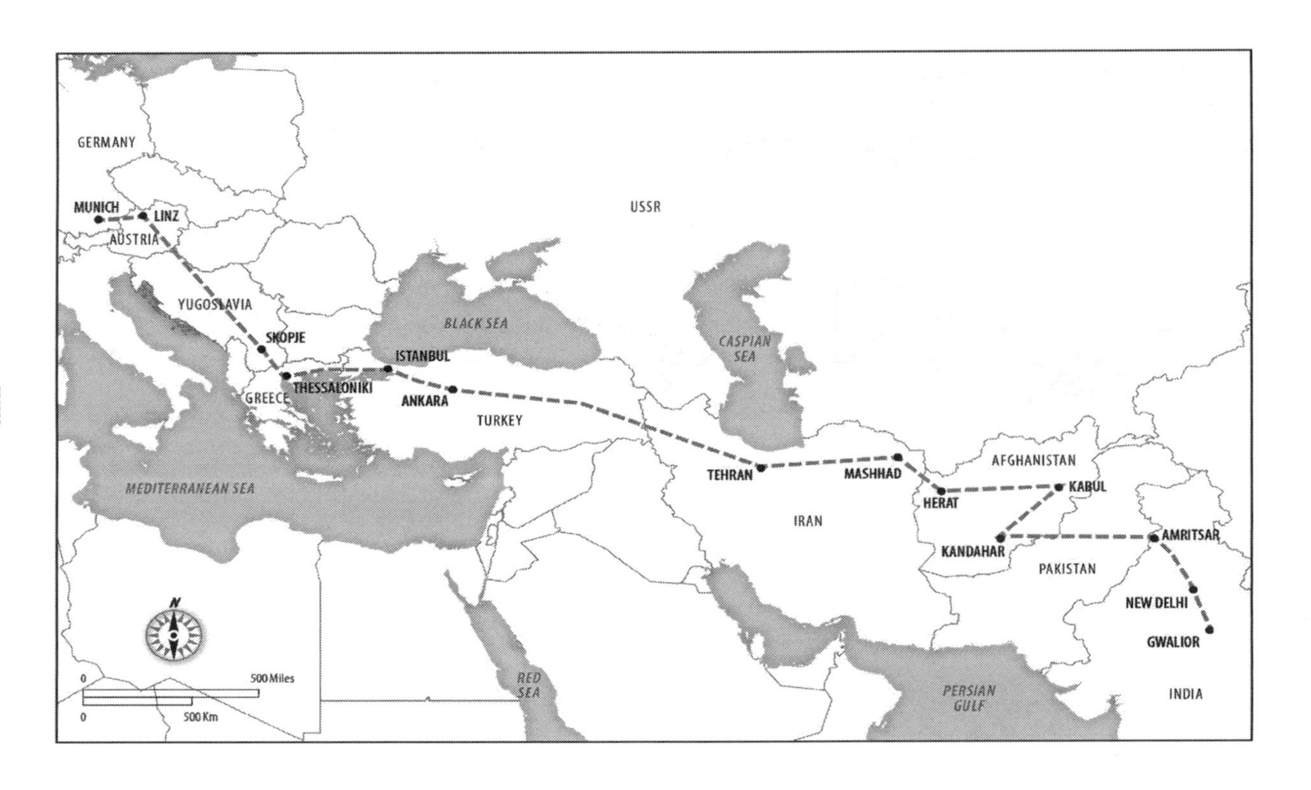
GERMANY
MUNICH
LINZ
AUSTRIA
USSR
YUGOSLAVIA
SKOPJE
BLACK SEA
ISTANBUL
THESSALONIKI
GREECE
ANKARA
TURKEY
CASPIAN SEA
MEDITERRANEAN SEA
TEHRAN
MASHHAD
AFGHANISTAN
HERAT
KABUL
IRAN
KANDAHAR
AMRITSAR
PAKISTAN
NEW DELHI
GWALIOR
N
0
500 Miles
0
500 Km
RED SEA
PERSIAN GULF
INDIA

PART ONE ✵ PRADEEP

Gwalior, India, 1965

I BELIEVED IN FREEDOM, FREE to marry who I wanted, to earn money doing what I loved and to own a home. I desired a good quality of life. But this was India, a country that suffered from a heavy population, air pollution, and government corruption. Poverty and chaos prevailed. It was not going to be easy. Not having the means to fulfill my basic needs in life was demeaning to me. I was a restless ambitious teenager, disillusioned and dissatisfied with my country and frustrated with its traditions. I wanted more out of life than what Gwalior had to offer. My parents called me a rebel.

I thought about these things as I sat on the rooftop of my parents' house. It was a single-story brick house where I lived with my parents and six siblings, I being the third child. It was a modest house near the railroad station. My father, Hari Ratan Parashar, worked as a railway station master, a well-respected job and my mother, Yamuna devi, was a schoolteacher.

In the mornings I had the habit of sitting up on the rooftop, drinking chai and watching the activities below me.

The dirt road filled up with people walking, pushing carts filled with vegetables for the market and children running to school dressed in their uniforms of blue and white. This morning was unusually hot, and I had to use my handkerchief to wipe the sweat off my brow. As I relaxed in the sultry air, I noticed my friend, Ashoo, rushing by.

"Hey, Ashoo!" I yelled, "Where are you going?"

Nearly out of breath, Ashoo yelled back, "I'm going to my English lesson with the Peace Corps Volunteers. I'm late! You should come too. Come with me tomorrow." Then he disappeared into the crowd.

I studied English in school, but to study with an American was too good an opportunity to pass up. My older brother, Vimal, once told me "What matters most in learning the English language was the content. It must be clearly conveyed and understood."

Even though the sun hung low in the sky, the early morning heat penetrated into everything and everyone.

I wiped my moist face again, brushed my damp, black hair from my eyes and thought about Ashoo's invitation to join him tomorrow. If a person wanted to advance his knowledge, ie. work for the government or be hired for any other type of public profession, a good understanding of the English language was a necessity.

Yes, being tutored in English by an American would be an excellent idea.

Gwalior was a small vibrant city, 198 miles south of New Delhi in the State of Madhya Pradesh. It was known for its many historical sites: the Man Singh Palace, Jaivilas Palace, and for the Gwalior Fort which dominated the city. The majority of people were Hindus and spoke Hindi. Like most of India, Gwalior suffered from over-population. In sections of the city drinking water was tainted from ground pollution and lack of plumbing. Because the banking system was not handled properly, people buried their money, hid it under mattresses or stuffed it in their clothing. Young adults could not marry whom they wanted. Marriages were arranged by parents.

India's society was defined by a caste system, which was made up of four divisions: Brahman, being the highest status, Kshatriya, Vaishys, and Sudra. The lowest were "the Untouchables," eventually called "Dalits," the outcasts of society.

My family belonged to the Brahman caste, but if I wanted to work as an unskilled laborer, I would be disgraced, along with my entire family. That would be a job for someone in the Sudra's caste. Brahmans worked as teachers, leaders, or government officials. The military and generals were the responsibility of the Kshatriyas and agriculture and raising cattle were left for the Vaishys.

I believed that the caste system and its strict rules inhibited choice and growth.

In addition, most people in India preferred fair-skinned Indians. Lighter skin color was considered more beautiful and was associated with a higher status. Fair-skinned people often got better jobs than dark-skinned people. This was not racism, it was "colorism," and of course, it wasn't fair. My skin was on the dark side and I wanted some day to have a high paying job with high status. I didn't want to be held back by the color of my skin.

In 1947, the nation celebrated, not because I was born, but because India had gained its freedom from the British. India had been ruled by the British for two hundred years and at midnight on August 15, 1947, Great Britain closed the door on India and walked away, leaving the country with cricket, hockey, and tea. They introduced the English language, the Indian Railways, the Postal Service, and improved road conditions. Even though India gained its independence, corruption arose throughout the country. Battles between Muslims and Hindus continued with more force. The Congress Party and the Muslim League could not agree on what they wanted, and the Muslims did not want to live under a perpetual Hindu-majority rule. Pakistan split from India and turmoil took over the country.

My family struggled along with our fellow Indians in the aftermath of the British Raj. For a time we lived with no electricity and shared a common toilet with other families in the neighborhood. Once a week, my mother would stand in line at the government-controlled shop to pick up food, wheat, rice, and other grains.

When I was old enough, I walked with my older brother a quarter of a mile to a well to draw water. We filtered the water through a thin cloth into drinking pots made of clay. After the pots were filled, and before we left for home, we would always feed the squirrels and birds. We would walk home carrying the pots on our shoulders or heads. As a reward, mother served us *marsala chai*, tea with milk, ginger and sugar.

Working for the railway was not an easy job. Most of the time my father would be sent to another district and could not live at home with his family. My mother found this difficult and she would relocate us to wherever he was working. I found it hard to make friends and to adjust to the new school. It interfered with my learning and I spent much of my time alone.

When we finally settled in Gwalior, my mother became a teacher in a remote village. She lived there during the week and returned home on the weekends. Now, we had both parents off working, and my siblings and I were left alone to fend for ourselves. Because there were seven of us of various ages, we looked after each other. We cleaned, cooked, and helped each other get ready for school.

Even with my mother working, we lived simply and by the time I reached high school, I felt I should be of some use. I began tutoring children in the neighborhood with their studies and soon earned enough to purchase a radio, a fan, and to help pay for electricity. The best thing was the fan. Temperatures during the day could go as high as 120 degrees! We welcomed our neighbors on those hot days and we stayed cool together.

In my community, having a bicycle commanded respect. I wanted a bicycle desperately, so I could gain the respect of the other boys. Having a bike was considered a luxury. Once a week, my father would give me snack money and instead of spending it on sweets, I saved my *paises* coins until I had enough money to buy my own bike. It was my pride and joy!

I had another reason for wanting this bicycle, and that was to help my older sister, Kusum. She had a four and a half mile walk to school every day on a crowded, dusty dirt road. Cars and trucks, cows, wild dogs, and the heat made the journey dangerous. On a bicycle, I could get her to school faster and keep her safe.

Kusum and four other girls were the only ones who studied science/biology at the Padma Vidhyalaya, a Maharaja's girl's school. Our family was very proud of her. However, when my sisters, like most women in India, were between the ages of 20 and 25 years old, they were expected to get married and they didn't have a choice. The marriage is arranged by the parents. The prospects of Kusum proceeding with a profession in biology was almost impossible. My parents were obligated to find their daughter a suitable husband, an Indian tradition. It would be a disgrace to both families if she or the husband refused.

When a marriage was arranged a dowry *dahel* was required. Parents gave their daughter jewelry. money, land, car or other fancy gifts as an offering to the husband and his family. Some families "donated" their daughters to the families because they could not afford the gifts.

Over the years, I noticed that my father, uncles and other men were free to gather outside of the home, such as a public park or a chai stall. Whereas, the social circle for women was limited to close relatives and other neighboring women within their homes. I saw no equality between men and women and women were treated like "baggage" in India. These memories surfaced through my consciousness and sparked the reality of my beliefs.

I swatted at the annoying flies that were buzzing around my head and poured another cup of chai. Perhaps the heat affected me, but the urgency to make something of myself suddenly emerged. I could see no future for me in India and for many years had had the dream of leaving. How and when and where were questions that surfaced frequently.

The next day, filled with anticipation, I walked with Ashoo to meet the American tutor.

The American Peace Corps

DAN CUMMINGS HAD ARRIVED in India in the heat of the summer along with other volunteers from the American Peace Corps. He came from Chicago, Illinois and was assigned to teach at Miss Hills School, a government aided private school.

He greeted me with a warm smile and a strong handshake. He was a tall, lanky fellow, with an easy manner, yet energetic. I liked him immediately.

I found out that several boys in the area had become curious about the Americans arriving in Gwalior and gathered around their living quarters. The volunteers welcomed the boys and soon after, began helping them with their English.

The meetings at Dan's house were casual and informal, focusing on dialogue and questions and answers. I took these lessons seriously and my English improved greatly.

Dan and his roommate Gus received so many books from friends and American organizations that they didn't know what to do with them. They soon transformed a room in their house and created a library where the books would be available for anyone in Gwalior to use.

Dan wanted to improve his Hindi, so he asked me to tutor him, and at the same time assist him with the library. I was delighted. The arrangement worked well. We organized the books on shelves and after several weeks opened the library to the public. My father visited the library and was impressed with what we had accomplished. He suggested we join the Indo-American Friendship and Cultural Society. It was a newly formed non-government, non-political organization in Gwalior to be connected with the United States Information Service in New Delhi. The goal was to enhance the cultural exchange between these two great countries.

My father suggested that the library should represent other countries, as well. Because my father supported the Communist Party, he suggested subscribing to two popular Russian magazines, "Soviet Land" and "Soviet Nari" (Women).

Hari Parashar was very proud of India's young democracy and as a government employee, it was his duty to support the Constitution in spite of racial, caste, and sectarian differences. However, he leaned toward a more Communistic view. A few trustworthy local intellectuals who were active members of the Communist Party of India (Marxist) frequently held long meetings at our house to discuss the political drama nation-wide. One day Vimal came home with a copy of "The Little Red Book," written in 1964 by Mao Zedong (Tse-Tung), Chairman of the Communist Party of China. Owning this book in India was illegal and considered dangerous. Instead of being pleased, my father was furious. Vamil could have exposed the family and Hari could have lost his job.

Dan had a great influence on me, not only as a great tutor but by giving me a picture of what American life was like: I could buy a car, have my own apartment, choose a job, date, and marry for love. A picture of freedom. The thoughts of leaving India became stronger.

I read everything I could get my hands on. Soon, I learned to communicate and read at a high level. I watched Hollywood movies whenever I had the chance and would repeat the dialogues over and over again until I could repeat every word perfectly. Because of this, I acquired the ability to mimic different accents, which amused my friends.

Gus, Dan's roommate, was assigned to oversee a poultry farm owned and operated by the Secretary of the Maharaja of Gwalior and I volunteered to assist him. Gus grew up on a farm in Wisconsin. He was strong, robust and eager to work. He wore his golden hair short which matched his well-kept beard. I noticed that he never took off his sunglasses which sat on his thick black eyeglasses. This combination appeared much too large for his narrow face. He certainly didn't go around unnoticed.

To my advantage, Gus had no interest in speaking Hindi, so that meant I could speak English while I was working with him. We spent long hours on the farm feeding the animals and tending to the gardens. That meant I had plenty of time to babble along in my new-found language.

The volunteers often called upon me to translate for them. On occasion, they would get lost while venturing out to visit another town or while sightseeing around Gwalior, and I would listen to their stories of woe. I felt badly when this happened and offered to be their tour guide. This way, they would no longer wander off in the wrong direction.

There had been a rumor circulating around Gwalior that the Peace Corps Volunteers were engaged in activities connected to the CIA (Central Intelligence Agency). If so, this could threaten India's national security. The officials began to eye me suspiciously because it was known that I spent a great deal of time volunteering with the Peace Corps.

President Kennedy established the Peace Corps in 1961, in order to expose American youth to the customs, traditions, and languages of other countries. This would result in broadening their knowledge of the world and creating good relationships among nations. Foreign countries would request the presence of the Peace Corps and express what assistance they needed. The Indian government invited them to help with education, the building of schools and roads, and to assist with farming.

It was surprising to me to hear of this accusation, because the Prime Minister, Jawaharlal Nehru, was pro-American and signed the treaty with President Kennedy to obtain aid for the volunteer project.

I was dismayed when I heard rumors that some of my friends questioned my loyalty to India. Needless to say, I ignored them and continued working with my American friends.

In 1967, it was time for the volunteers to leave. The stint in India lasted only two years so Dan and Gus had to return to the USA. The accomplishments of the Peace Corps in Gwalior had been successful and appreciated. I felt a bond with Dan and Gus, learned much from them and it was hard to say goodbye. We promised to keep in touch.

Soon after they had departed, an ex-Peace Corps volunteer arrived. His name was Pete Wilkins.

Pete had spent two years with the Peace Corps in Punjab. He had returned to India with a grant from Cornell University to work on his PHD in anthropology under the Indian Studies Program. Pete had heard that I had worked with the previous volunteers and contacted me requesting that I work with him in his research. I accepted and was delighted to learn that I would be paid sixty dollars a month (the equivalent of a District Magistrate's earnings!).

Pete's research project took place in the remote village of Panihar, fifteen miles southwest of Gwalior. The purpose of his thesis was to learn what had changed in this village regarding kinship and social structure, and whether it was due to intrusion or to urban contact; how did this village affect the city, of Gwalior and how did the city affect the village of Panihar.

My responsibilities included interviewing the village people, asking them how often they visited the city to shop, see friends or relatives, and how often did the city people come to the village to shop and visit family and friends.

I needed to acquaint myself with Panihar and its people, so I moved into the village. It was easier for me to get the information and then translate directly to Pete.

I was a young man, five foot eight or nine, slight stature, nice white teeth and liked to dress in style. I wore pressed pants and button-down shirts. As soon as I arrived in the village, I realized that the local people who dressed in traditional garb, might not trust me nor want to talk with me if I dressed in my stylish clothes. I looked foreign, perhaps a threat. I changed to wearing a *kurta*, a long shirt and *pajamas*, loose pants. As a result, I felt more comfortable and I believe the villagers were more comfortable talking and confiding in me.

Gathering the information with the villagers went well, but Pete discovered some things didn't make sense. "Why was this faction splitting? Why was the land being sold? Why was the composition of the local politics changing?

We were shocked to discover that these changes were happening because of kidnappings. Since the twelfth century the area had been ruled by *dacoits*, the Rajputs. This renegade group considered killing and kidnapping a "sport." They were born to be warriors and to rule. They did not want that to change. The Brahmins in the village, on the other hand, were prestigious and did not want to be ruled in this manner any longer. They wanted this "sport" to stop.

Pete concluded: "The kidnappings changed the social composition and economic alignment within the village. Kidnapping was a practical way to redistribute resources with the ransoms they received. The various castes had gangs, but the bandits weren't really bandits. They considered themselves to be Bagis, rebels against injustice. Their injustice lay in their perception that they were no longer special, and they were trying to recapture their old ways."

After eighteen months and tons of paperwork, Pete's dissertation project was completed, and he returned to the USA. I wasn't sure what to do with myself after Pete left. I had experienced hard work with brilliant, innovative people for over three years. I spoke excellent English, had made good friends and had energy to do much more. My future stood before me. These were my thoughts:

Without the American Peace Corps in Gwalior, I had lost a good part of my dream. My mind was processing what was happening outside of me and inside of me at all times.

Friends thought I was anti-India because of my involvement with the Americans. The library we had established consisting of thousands of books, mostly American books, were donated to various schools and collage libraries. The words in these books had meaning to me and constantly created new ideas in my mind. I was obsessed with reading.

My heart pounded, my lungs inhaled and exhaled laboriously. My muscles tightened, all with the excitement of the written words. Inside my body and brain, all the systems that make me who I am, worked overtime. Without my friends from the Peace Corps, I now felt abandoned, ostracized by my friends and family, anxious. I kept telling myself, "I don't belong here." I was going insane.

The World Travel Bureau, 1970

I KNEW MY PARENTS WOULD reject the idea of me leaving the country; they had great expectations for their children, especially for the boys. Becoming a doctor, lawyer, or an engineer would make the family proud and they would gain much respect in the community. It worried my parents to know that I was not interested in any of these professions. I learned very early in life that "money is the only thing Indians think about" and my parents were no exception.

I had listened intently to the stories the Americans had shared about their lives in the States. They had freedom and opportunities that I could never have here in India. I desired this lifestyle.

Over the last three years, I had developed self-confidence, mastered the English language, understood techniques for research, and loved being around people.

After several weeks of thinking, pacing and drinking lots of chai, I realized that associating with an international group of people might work for me. I knew India and its history well, so being a tour guide sounded like a possibility. I could assist English speaking tourists as well as fellow Indians with their travel plans.

"Why not open a travel business?" I concluded.

"With my earnings, I could leave India."

Motivated, I applied for a passport, which in India was a highly regarded document. I contacted the proper authorities to obtain a license to open a private tourism business in Gwalior. I paid the fees and found an office in Hotel Hemsons, a small but busy Indian-style hotel where Indian tourists stayed.

"The World Travel Bureau" was born!

The office space was a bit cramped, but room enough for two small wooden chairs, a simple desk and a swivel chair. I placed a pad of paper and two pens on the desktop and hooked up a phone. I tacked posters of Taj Mahal, the Red Fort, and the Temples of Khajuraho on the walls. I felt pleased as I looked around me. It looked professional and I felt confident I could generate and promote tourism in my city.

Within six months, I had accomplished what I had set out to do. I had acquired many satisfied customers, preparing their travel itineraries and helping them with their travel documents, domestic and international. However, clients did not come every day. That was always worrisome.

Most mornings, before opening the office, I would sit alone and eat my breakfast at the hotel restaurant. One morning, the hotel manager interrupted me, saying there was a couple waiting for me in my office. I took one last sip of my chai and dashed off to meet my prospective clients.

As I headed to the office, I assumed the couple would be Indian, but it turned out they were Westerners who looked like "well-seasoned travelers."

"*Namaste.* My name is Pradeep Parashar. Please have a seat," I said, as I gestured toward the two chairs. "How can I help you?"

The young woman spoke up, "My name is Carol Moore, and this is my boyfriend Chris Allen. We've been traveling for quite a long time on our own and now we'd like a tour guide to show us some interesting areas of central India. Could you help us?"

"Yes, I certainly can get you the information you may need. Are you American?" I asked curiously.

"I am American, and Chris is from Canada," she answered and continued her story. "We have been traveling by car, which we picked up in Frankfurt, Germany. From there we drove to Kabul, Afghanistan and continued to Lahore, Pakistan, where we left our car in a parking garage," Carol carefully explained.

"We were nervous about driving a car in India," added Chris, who looked nervous while sitting in a chair, "because we read about the terrible road conditions and irresponsible drivers. We also didn't want to drive with cows, oxen, and elephants randomly walking in the middle of the road. I read a statistic that there are more road deaths in India than any other country in the world!"

"Curvy roads, people not using signals, and horns blasting out of control, were things we knew we couldn't deal with," Carol confessed with a laugh.

I listened, amused, "You made a good choice!"

I took out a copy of the "Lonely Planet" guidebook and suggested they look through it for ideas of where they might want to go. I ordered chai for my guests as they began their search.

Carol was an attractive young woman from Tucson, Arizona, in her late twenties, tall, slender, with long blonde hair and a happy personality. Chris, coming from outside Toronto, Canada, was of medium height and build and had a thin face with a thin mustache. I noticed he fidgeted with his hair, combing the brown strands away from his face with his fingers. The couple were casual, "hippie-like," and easy to talk with. I liked them immediately. While they were looking through the guidebook, Chris took out a joint.

"Can I smoke?" he asked.

"Go ahead, no problem" I replied, though a little surprised at his request.

Smoking hash was not something I normally did, but I was open to the spontaneity of these travelers. Soon the joint was being passed around.

Within less than an hour, and fully feeling the effects of the drug, they had their trip mapped out. It would last two weeks and I, as their tour escort, would arrange everything. I would receive two dollars a day. We would travel by bus and train to Orccha, Khajuraho, Agra and back to Gwalior. I knew these places well and drew up an itinerary that would give them a general picture of India's history, culture and cuisine.

After we had finished the arrangements, they asked if I were free for the afternoon to escort them around Gwalior. I had no other plans and earning some extra money sounded good. We set off to view the Sun Temple, Gwalior Fort, the city's most magnificent monument, and other museums.

Early the next day, we boarded the Taj Express for Orccha, a medieval city in the state of Madhya Pradesh, located on the Betwa River. For three days we wandered the streets, talking, smoking joints, absorbing history. We sat by the flowing river and drank chai at the outside stalls. The area was not over-populated with tourists, so it was easy to get around. A few shops were scattered around the Rama Temple and other smaller monuments. On the third day, we crammed our bags and ourselves into a small rickety "auto rickshaw" (a three wheeled open-air cart with an engine in the back). After a bumpy, jerky ride to the bus station, we boarded a bus for Khajuraho. This village was made up of, at least, twenty enormous temples constructed between 950-1050 AD. The elaborate structures of stone were carved meticulously by artisans who in their work depicted life in every form.

Carol, Chris, and I walked these streets in awe of the temples which emitted such strength and glory. Even though I'd seen this all before, it still amazed me.

After a few days, we caught a bus to Jhansi where we caught the crowded Punjab Mail Train headed for Agra in the state of Uttar Pradesh. It is here that the majestic Taj Mahal stands. The Mogul monument, sitting along the Yamuna River, was built in memory of Mumtaz Mahal, wife of the Emperor Shah Jahan. She died in childbirth in 1632 after having fourteen children. The monument, representing love and heartbreak, was completed in 1653.

My friends and I walked around the gardens viewing this magnificent monument of passion, honoring the past and feeling a sense of serenity.

Time was running out and Carol and Chris needed to head back to Gwalior in order to plan and pack for their trip to New Delhi. From there, they would travel to Pakistan, fetch their car and continue on to Germany.

They thanked me for leading them on a safe trip filled with good food and cheap hotels. A close friendship had developed and on top of this, we agreed that we had been great traveling companions.

One night when we were hanging out, I shared with them my feelings of discontentment with my country, and how I wanted to leave India to find a better life.

Carol and Chris had talked about their lives with their schooling, apartments, cars, and travels, and once again I got the impression that life outside India was filled with new and greater opportunities. Before we parted, they asked,

"Would you like to travel to West Germany with us? We will pay for your food and sleeping accommodations. You won't have any expenses."

Without a second thought, I accepted the offer.

West Germany, an industrial country, sounded like a perfect place to find work and Indian citizens did not require an entry visa.

First, Carol and Chris would need to go to New Delhi. Carol needed to pick up money being sent to the American Express Banking Service and to claim a package at the Gole Market Post Office containing contact lens solution, both being sent by her mother. After, they would continue by bus to Lahore where they would pick up their car.

Several emotions tumbled through my mind: excitement, fear, and skepticism. I knew that my parents would not approve of this sudden, unthinkable idea of leaving home.

"How will you pay for this?" they inquired.

"Germany is too far away. When would we see you again?" Mother desperately asked.

"Who are these people you'd be traveling with and can you trust them?" Father asked in a concerned tone.

"No, no, this would not be possible!" My parents firmly opposed their son.

Their reaction was predictable, but I had a plan. I would invite Carol and Chris for dinner, with the hope, that after meeting the couple, my parents would change their minds. They agreed to the dinner invitation.

Mamaji ordered the children to help clean the house. She took out her best plates and cups and went to the market to buy the freshest vegetables. My mother took special care in preparing a traditional vegetarian meal of *matar paneer* (green peas and cheese curry), *pooris* (deep fried puffy bread), *kheer* (rice pudding) and *pumpkin raita* (pumpkin and yogurt).

My family greeted my guests with warmth and respect, and Chris and Carol appreciated the delicious feast. After dinner my father and Chris discussed in English the route to Germany, the time it would take to get there (six to eight weeks), and other details. Chris explained to my father that he and Carol would pay for everything, including "transient visas" which were always available at the borders. Chris explained how gracious a tour guide I had been, and that they wanted to reciprocate by taking me with them to Germany.

The dinner plan had worked, at least with my father. He felt more at ease with the travel plans and with the people I'd be traveling with. My mother who was cleaning in the kitchen, was not aware of the conversation, and that her husband agreed with her son's trip. She was still against it.

Hopefully, my father would be able to convince my mother to agree. In my mind, I was going regardless of whatever my mother said. The next day I bought myself a custom-made sleeping bag, which took the stitcher five hours to make, and bought a lightweight backpack.

Chris, Carol and I met one more time to draw up a final

plan. They would go to New Delhi, check into a hotel, pick up their items and leave a note at the American Express Office explaining where they were staying. I would join them at the hotel in a week and we'd continue to Pakistan. I needed this time to pack, say good-by to family and friends and get the vaccinations needed for my trip. I had arranged to stay with my uncle, Kishen, in New Delhi while my travel documents were prepared. However, my parents still had a few concerns.

My mother who had five sons and two daughters, complained about losing another child. Kusum, the eldest daughter, had moved to London with her husband two years ago. Now a second family member was planning on leaving, too. My youngest brother, Sunil who was in the third grade, was also concerned about me leaving. Every day I would give him a coin. Where was that coin going to come from now?

The night before I was to leave Gwalior, I heard my parents discussing the turmoil they were experiencing. They knew that I would need some money for my personal use and wanted to give me some, however, they only had a few hundred rupees in the house and no other savings.

"Why don't we borrow some money from our neighbor?" Father suggested to my mother.

Pointing a wagging finger at her husband, she yelled, "Absolutely not! You have lost control of your son and as a result, we will lose another family member."

Father spoke softly to his wife. "Calm down, Yamuna. You have five sons. If one of them disappears tomorrow, let's say he died, you would never see him again. In that situation, we would have to arrange his funeral. So, why don't we arrange to pay for Pradeep's funeral in advance?"

He calculated the cost of a Hindu funeral. The total amount came to $196.50

"If we don't give him the money, we will feel guilty because we turned away from our social obligation." Because she knew that her family and his would be disgraced, she had no choice but to agree to his request.

In the morning, while the family members were gathered together drinking their morning chai, my father politely suggested to my mother that she go next door to their neighbor and ask to borrow at least $160.00. In less than ten minutes, she returned with the money in hand. Their $30.00 was added and with the spare change lying around the house, they had gathered the full $196.50.

With tears in her eyes, mother handed the "funeral money" over to me. I was reluctant to take it, but she slipped it into my shirt pocket. She gave me a warm hug, and I knew I had her blessing. I was free to go.

The Punjab Mail Train arrived at the Gwalior Railway Station at 12:45 p.m. My father, Sunil, and I arrived fifteen minutes early. Mother had made me snacks and a lunch. My father had obtained a "family journey pass" to New Delhi for me, a free pass which is a privilege only for railway employees. As we waited, I noticed my father deep in thought. He didn't speak and took a short walk along the platform.

When he returned, he looked at me with sad eyes and said he and mother will miss me and they will look forward to my letters wherever I may be. I bowed down respectfully and touched my father's feet, to receive his blessing. In return he placed his hand upon my head and blessed me.

I picked up my things, hugged my worried looking little brother and boarded the train. When the train started moving, I had a feeling I had forgotten something. As I looked out the window, I focused on Sunil. I realized I hadn't given him his coin today. I frantically searched my pockets. I found one and tossed it out the window, yelling to Sunil to pick it up. I watched him race toward the bouncing coin and catch it. With a big smile, he vigorously waved good-by to his big brother.

New Delhi, January, 1971

I SETTLED INTO MY SEAT, closing my eyes, and let my body be soothed by the rhythm of the moving train. My mind wandered to visions of the future, the past, to my family and friends. I was on my way to New Delhi, meeting with the couple who were about to make my dream of leaving India come true. I wanted to yell out, to everyone on the train, "This is IT, the BIGGEST event in my life!" But I didn't. I just put a big grin on my face and chuckled.

Five hours later, the train arrived in New Delhi. I grabbed my bags and headed for my uncle's house. Uncle Kishan, who worked for the Central Bureau of Investigation, was curious about my unexpected travel plans and showed concern about the people I'd be traveling with. I explained how I met Carol Moore and Chris Allen and told him he had no reason for concern. My uncle's main question was why I wanted to leave India in the first place.

"What about your education?" he asked.

"I can get an education anywhere, but this opportunity might be offered only once," I explained. That was true and my uncle refrained from further questioning.

The next morning, while I drank chai with my cousins, Uncle Kishan called me into the study where he was reading the "Times of India." He pointed out an article in which a Carol Moore had been arrested the day before at the Gole Market Post Office. Apparently, she had disobeyed a postal authority's instruction and caused a disturbance.

I asked him for directions to the Mandir Marg Police Station, where the article said she was being held and raced out the door. When I arrived, Chris greeted me and reported that the bail was set at one hundred dollars. Carol assumed the money sent by her mother would take care of the bail, but the money had not yet arrived which created quite a dilemma. I immediately reached into my pocket, took out a hundred dollars of my" funeral money" and paid the bail. Within an hour, she was free to go, and a court hearing was scheduled for the following month.

Before Chris had gone to the police station, he had informed the US Embassy of the episode. After Carol had been released, he called the embassy back to let them know that she was free and leaving the police station.

Relieved, the US Consul invited us to dinner that evening at the embassy compound. He wanted to hear the whole story.

That afternoon, I consulted a local lawyer. He advised me that if Carol were leaving India in a week or so, she need not worry about missing the court hearing, because the charge was a minor one.

During dinner with the US Consul, Carol explained what happened.

"My mother had sent a package of contact lens solution two weeks ago. When I went to the post office to claim my package, I noticed it was damaged. I thought that some of the liquid had spilled out and asked if I could check the package before paying the excise duty. The postal clerk refused to let me examine the package, and without thinking, I grabbed the package from his hand. He and I wrestled with the parcel, causing quite a ruckus, and he called the police."

After we left the consulate, we continued to celebrate Carol's release in a quaint little restaurant where I spent more of my "funeral money." At the end of the evening, I had $70.00 left.

The following day, I applied for the Iranian and Afghanistan visas and picked them up within a few hours. The next day I applied for a visa at the Pakistan Embassy, which I was told would be ready at 1:00 p.m. However, a couple of hours before my visa was to be issued, an agitated mob of several hundred locals surrounded the Pakistan Embassy. The Indian people were outraged, because an Indian passenger plane had been hijacked and set on fire in Lahore. In retaliation, the unruly crowd threw rocks at the embassy and created a riot. I saw this going on and hid behind a building to avoid the chaos while I waited for 1:00.

Then, an announcement came over a loudspeaker, "No visas will be issued to any Indian passport holder until further notice. Effective immediately. Anyone who has applied for a visa today can pick up their passport at 5:00 p.m. at the back-office window No. 3."

Irritated and annoyed at this inconvenience, I went back to my uncle's. At 5:00, I picked up my passport and walked to the hotel where Chris and Carol were staying. I explained what happened at the embassy and we sat down to map out a new plan. Carol suggested I take a plane to Kabul, Afghanistan and avoid Pakistan all together. I liked that idea.

Chris and Carol would get their money from American Express, go to Lahore to pick up their car, and drive to Kabul. Carol gave me instructions on how to get to Hotel Mustafa in Kabul where they would be staying. They knew the manager, Mahmood, and I was to explain to him that they would be arriving in a few days and would pay my bill.

The next morning, I walked from my uncle's house to the Ariana Afghan Airline office on Connaught Place. I noticed there was a flight to Kabul twice a week from Amritsar. A round trip ticket cost fifty dollars and fifty cents and a one-way ticket cost fifty dollars. The ticket agent suggested the round trip, just in case I had to come home. I thought that was good advice and bought the round-trip ticket. After paying for the visas and the airline ticket, I had $10.00 left.

Amritsar was a border town between India and Pakistan, and from New Delhi, it was an overnight journey by train. That evening I boarded the train, which cost eight dollars, leaving me with two dollars in my pocket.

When I reached the airport, I checked in and sat down. Right before take-off, an announcement was made that the flight to Kabul had been canceled. The next available flight would be in three days.

I stood up in disgust and waited for further instructions. An airline official issued a hotel voucher. At the expense of the airline, I stayed at a nice hotel, food included, until my flight departed. On the third day, anticipating a flight to Kabul, I was told the plane would be flying to Kandahar instead. From there I would board another plane to Kabul. The fare was $1.00.

I would have $1.00 left! Practically broke and certainly helpless if another crisis occurred.

On the third day, I boarded a ninety-seater Boeing aircraft. To my surprise, there were only four passengers. Piles of boxes and parcels occupied the rest of the seats. I had never flown before, and had to admit, I was nervous. I didn't know what to expect.

The plane rumbled as it took off, I closed my eyes, held on tightly to the arm rests and chanted a Hindu prayer. Once the plane leveled off and I calmed down, I looked out the window. At 29,000 feet in the air, I saw a new perspective of the world. At that moment, I knew I would be involved in the airline industry. I imagined me setting up a tourist business, the one selling tickets and receiving a hefty commission.

I sat back, relaxed, and sank into my reverie.

When the plane landed, the passengers were informed that the flight to Kabul would leave the following day at 6 a.m. Again, plans had changed, and again, I was provided with a hotel room. The flight took an hour. Upon my arrival in Kabul, I had to show my International Vaccination Certificate, which had been issued at the Municipal Authority of Gwalior. I was told it was invalid. Frustrated, I had to relent in receiving yet another vaccination. At least I had made it to Kabul and would soon meet up with my friends.

Afghanistan

CHICKEN STREET WAS A winding, crowded, and dusty road filled with vendors, shops, restaurants, and hotels. After a half hour walk, I found Hotel Mustafa. I introduced myself to the manager, Mahmood, and explained the situation concerning Chris and Carol. He remembered them and agreed to accommodate me. He was friendly and led me to a small but clean room. I waited anxiously for four days, and when they drove up to the hotel, I was relieved.

However, there seemed to be some friction between the two of them. Evidently, on their way to Kabul, they picked up a French hitchhiker who paid more attention to Carol than to Chris. There appeared to be some flirtation going on and Chris became jealous. He caused a scene, which infuriated Carol. Sensing there was a problem, the Frenchman quickly departed.

Carol did not want anything more to do with Chris and decided to take a bus to Munich, instead of driving with him. Chris begged her to change her mind.

I couldn't believe our glorious plan had just fizzled away.

Now, in our separate rooms, we prepared for our separate trips. I didn't know what Chris and I were going to do. What was going to happen to Carol's car?

Carol had promised my parents that she and Chris would accompany me to Munich, and since she was now taking the bus, Carol thought it would help if the car was given to me. This way, she'd be meeting half of her responsibility.

The truth was, I had never driven a car before, nor did I have a driver's license. Nevertheless, the next day, papers were transferred, and I became an owner of a Ford Taurus Station Wagon!

Because Chris needed to get to Munich, he offered to drive and manage the journey for me. I knew I had to depend upon him.

Before our departure, I met with Carol for coffee and she apologized for the messy situation that occurred. As we sat talking, she reached into her handbag and handed me $30.00 and a ring. The ring was constructed of white gold inlaid with three small diamonds, delicate and lovely. Before Carol left Tucson, her mother purchased this ring for her daughter, in case Carol planned to get married some day. It was valued at eleven hundred dollars. Carol felt guilty about deserting me, and thought if I ever needed financial help, I could sell the ring. I didn't know what to say, except "Thank you," and graciously accepted her gifts.

Carol bought a one-way bus ticket to Munich which was scheduled to leave the hotel at six a.m., Saturday morning. Chris did not want her to leave and believed he could find a way to make her stay. One of his schemes included paying a hotel employee two dollars to tell the bus driver she had already checked out and he should not wait for her. The employee deliberately forgot to tell Carol when the bus had arrived. She waited inside the hotel and noticed it was 7 a.m. and no one had come for her bags. A hotel guest informed her that the bus had already left. Perplexed and agitated for not being informed of the bus's arrival, she went to the manager to find out what happened. He did not know.

Curious, she started her own investigation and discovered what Chris had done. She was furious. She had just lost sixty dollars and now had to wait another week for the next bus.

Meanwhile, Chris dreamt up a plan for us.

"What if we bought eight kilos (17.6 pounds) of hash and hid it in the tubeless tires of our car? We could sell it in Amsterdam where it would bring in a quarter million dollars!"

I looked at him as if he were out of his mind, "I don't think that's a good idea, Chris," I said. "Carrying drugs, especially in the Middle Eastern countries, is a risky business. Border police in Iran can shoot you for smuggling drugs into their country, instantly, without a trial."

He bought the hash, anyway. I was annoyed and a bit fearful, but I needed him to drive me to Germany. I had no choice.

We drove out of the city with the eight kilos of hash and parked the car in an isolated place on the side of the road. Some shrubs and trees hid us so we could not be seen. We took all four tires off, one by one, and carefully stuffed two kilos in each tire. The hash came in solid 2"x 4" bars, like a bar of soap. They fit perfectly. When our deed was done, we secured the tires to the wheels and drove back to the hotel. As we entered, the desk clerk handed us a message from the

US Embassy which said our car needed to be inspected. The inspection would be at 10:00 in the morning the next day! "Park in front of Gate No. 2."

We were mystified, then alarmed. Why, so suddenly? Why did the car have to be inspected? Chris suspected that the dealer from whom he bought the hash was a secret informer for the embassy. No matter how the embassy found out, we had to clean out the four tires immediately. We needed to find another secretive place to deal with this unwanted situation.

We noticed a place across the street from our hotel called The 25 Hour Club which had a hose set up in a back parking lot. When the club closed at midnight, and the parking lot emptied, we could go in and clean out the tires.

In the darkness of the early morning, we cautiously drove the car to the back of the club. We worked quickly and quietly taking each tire off and placing the hash in a towel. We washed the tires thoroughly, re-bolted them and pumped them up with a hand pump that Chris had brought for the trip. By the time we were finished, there was absolutely no trace of hash residue anywhere. It took three hours and we were exhausted.

We stored the hash in Chris's room and later that morning, after little sleep, we drove to the embassy. At 10:00 we were parked in front of Gate No. 2. The inspection took no more than ten minutes. The car was cleared, and we were free to go. We, the clever smugglers, rushed back to the hotel, grabbed the towel with the hash wrapped in it, and drove out of town to the same spot where we had been the day before.

Once again we went through the tedious procedure of un-bolting the tires, filling each one with two blocks of hash, re-tightening the lugs and adjusting the air pressure.

Satisfied with our work, we hopped in the car, and Chris slowly steered the vehicle onto the highway. We drove back to the hotel to collect our belongings before check out time.

At 12:30 p.m., Carol, with new ticket in hand, waited in front of the hotel, determined not to miss the bus this time. Chris and I were packing the car in front of the hotel preparing for our trip. They would not speak to each other, but Chris continued to want her to come with us. When the bus pulled up, Chris moved the car behind it. His new plan consisted of following closely behind the bus, in hopes that along the way, Carol would get tired of sitting on an uncomfortable seat and want to join them. He kept the car running in order to be ready when the bus left.

Carol was aware of what was taking place and knew she needed to stop Chris from following her. She went to the grocery store nearby, bought a pound of sugar, and while Chris and I were half a block away smoking our cigarettes, she poured the sugar in the tank. Dropping the evidence on the sidewalk, she ran for the bus which was about to leave.

When we saw the bus slowly pulling out, we ran for the car. Chris saw the empty bag of sugar lying on the sidewalk and ran after the bus. He went ballistic. He grabbed the ladder on the back window, yelling, "Stop the bus! Stop the bus!" making quite a spectacle of himself. The bus driver, waving his arm out the window, yelled "Get off, Get off," and Carol was screaming, "Get him off, Get him off!" Finally, Chris, no longer able to hold on, fell to the pavement and the bus sped away, leaving behind a cloud of smoke.

Sugar in the gas tank was not a good thing. The rest of the day was spent at a garage having the tank cleaned, the bus and Carol long gone.

The following morning, we took off to the highway, ready to embark on our long journey to Germany. Within only 10 km, the car began to wobble and became difficult to maneuver. Chris pulled off to the side of the road to check the tires and discovered they were all flat!

We had been traveling at 85 kph on a rough pavement so we guessed that the rotation of the tires at a high speed had created extra heat. Apparently, the heat melted the hash which sucked up the air, resulting in flattening the tires. With four flat tires, we were going nowhere.

I found it comical to have gone through all this trouble and risk, only to have it all melt away. Actually, I felt relieved. Chris groaned in disbelief. Once again, we took the tires off. This time finding a gooey mess. The hash had turned into pebble shapes and had melted into the rubber. We scraped the gunk with our hands, sharp rocks, twigs, or whatever we could find. It was a slow process and we ended up with globs of hash. Obviously, in this state, the hash was worthless. I suggested we burn it, inhale and celebrate. Leaving it behind would have been a waste.

It was January and cold, so the fire we built served two purposes: warmth and getting stoned. For the first time in days, we relaxed, peacefully floating in the bliss of a hash high.

At sunrise, Chris, still high from the night before, took two of the damaged tires and hitchhiked to a gas station to be repaired. I stayed with the car and baggage. When he returned, he picked up the other two tires and set out again. Upon his second return we put the tires back on the car and continued on our journey.

A lot of money and time had been lost, but now we were not carrying an illegal substance which could have created serious problems at the border.

Soon after we were back on the road, we picked up two hitchhikers who were from Scandinavia.

Chris still thought about Carol with the hope that if he caught up to the bus, she might decide to continue the journey with us. He drove fast. After passing through Kandahar, he neglected to see the 25 kph speed sign. As he approached the sharp turn, traveling at 110 kph, he slammed on the brakes and the car slid off the road, rolled over on the roof and slid some more. Fortunately, the area was barren, and we didn't hit anything. Stunned and dazed, all four of us crawled out unscathed. In our state of shock, we managed to turn the car over. Amazingly, only two wheels on the right were noticeably bent, the rest of the car was intact. The two Scandinavians, still shaking, no longer wanted to stay with such an irresponsible driver, and walked away to hitch another ride.

Chris and I were left stranded on the side of the road, once again, with a car whose damaged wheels needed to be repaired. We took them off the car and Chris, grasping them awkwardly with one in each hand, headed to the highway to find a garage.

I was tired and sat down on the ground, leaning my back against the car. My mind wondered with doubtful thoughts of where this trip was headed. I hoped I would have good karma for the rest of my journey.

While deep in thought, I was startled by the presence of four Afghani men standing next to me. One carried a rifle and presented himself as a police officer. The others, who were talking amongst themselves, were dressed in long kaftans. Of course, I didn't know what they were saying, but it didn't sound promising. The man with the rifle motioned me to stand up and hand over my passport holder. When he opened it, he discovered the thirty dollars and Carol's ring. The scruffy intruder proceeded to stuff his findings in the pocket of his jacket. He nudged me with his rifle, indicating that I walk with them. I tried to resist.

"I'm waiting for my friend," I yelled, thinking they'd understand me better, "I cannot leave the car! Take the money, but I must stay here!" My pleading was in vain. Defeated, I walked silently with the kidnappers along a dirt road toward the mountain area. We walked, for what seemed like an hour, to a spot where several small huts stood. Circled around a glowing campfire squatted six or seven men and women eating dinner. We were offered food, but I declined. I did accept a cup of tea.

After everyone had eaten, the campers departed, and l was left alone with my kidnappers. They started arguing with each other, discussing, it seemed, my identity. I kept hearing the words "Maharaja of Gwalior." Because they had seen me with a nice car, a lot of money, and a beautiful ring, they must have surmised that I came from a wealthy Hindu family.

Around midnight, a dilapidated van driven by two disheveled bearded men drove up. I was shoved inside. There were no seats, therefore we had to sit on the floor. There were no windows and I could not see. At this point, I was terrified and could barely breathe. The van traveled for a long time, stopping and going over bumpy, curvy roads. I felt as though I might vomit. I knew that the Afghanis didn't understand Hindi, but I had to give it another try to explain who I was. In the dim light, I frantically tried motioning with my hands and using facial expressions to express my identity.

Surprisingly, the two drivers knew a little Hindi and when

the van stopped, they all agreed that I was not the young man they were looking for. I was more than shocked when they returned my passport holder and all of its contents. As soon as the back door of the van opened, I was free to go. I ran as fast as my feeble legs could carry me, and hoped I was headed in the direction of a city where I could get some help.

I reached a highway, stopped a couple who were walking along the road, and asked if there were a city near-by. They said the nearest city was Kandahar, about two to three km away, and pointed in the direction I needed to go.

First thing I wanted to do was to find a police station to explain what had happened to me and to request help in locating my car. When I found the police station, I began to explain my situation to an officer, but he rudely interrupted me and asked for my passport. He noticed that the visa had expired twenty-five days ago and told me there was a dollar a day penalty. Therefore, I had to pay him twenty-five dollars. After paying the fee, I had five dollars left.

Discouraged, I walked away. My growling stomach reminded me that I hadn't eaten for over twenty-four hours. I spent a dollar on food and asked the vendor how to get to the road to Herat, the border town between Afghanistan and Iran. "You can take a bus to the border which will cost two dollars," he replied and pointed toward the direction of the bus station. I bought the bus ticket. I now had two dollars left.

I figured while I was on the bus, if I saw my car, I would ask the bus driver to stop and I'd get out. Chris and I had agreed that if we became separated, for any reason, we would meet at the next border town on route. On route, I saw neither the car nor Chris and rode the bus all the way to Herat.

At the entry point, several officials boarded the bus to check everyone's documents. When they looked at my

International Vaccination Certificate, I was told that it was not valid because it did not have the internationally recognized stamp. I argued with them, explaining I had the vaccination in India and again in Kabul and it was written on my certificate. To the Iranian officials, it did not matter. It did not have the stamp they required, therefore, I needed to have the shot administered before I could enter Iran.

I walked over to the medical center and checked in. After having yet another vaccination, I was told it would take ten days to two weeks before the medical confirmation arrived from Tehran. I felt frustrated and discouraged. I had no choice but to stay at the center until the results came in.

One day, while looking out the window of the medical center, overlooking the street, I spotted my car. I asked the supervisor of the building if I could go out to let my friend know where I was. The answer was "NO." I never crossed paths with Chris nor my belongings again. On the eleventh day the report arrived. I was free to go.

With nothing, but my passport and two dollars, I walked over to the customs house. Gathered there were a small group of people who were traveling to Mashhad, Iran. A couple of people I recognized from the Mustafa Hotel. One of them was a Pakistani woman.

"Are you taking the bus to Mashhad?" She asked.

"I want to, but I don't have enough money for the ticket. I have a ring I could sell, then I'd have some money," I explained.

"Don't try to sell it here," she cautioned, "You would get a much better price if you sold it in a bigger city."

David, a young fellow who had also stayed at the hotel, overheard the conversation and offered to pay the three dollars for my bus fare. Good karma.

Iran

THE BUS WAS PACKED with passengers. Bags, coats, and other items were crammed onto the overhead racks. People scrambled to their seats, some quiet, others talking and laughing. Many languages could be overheard. Everyone settled into their seats and with the sound of grinding gears and a jerk, the bus took off. But within a short time, the bus stopped.

Two uniformed police boarded the bus. Apparently, it was a narcotic inspection check point. These inspectors were serious and lacked any sense of humor. They demanded eye contact from everyone, asking their name, nationality, and destination, and examined suspiciously all the visas and passports. All bags on the overhead racks were searched, as well as personal handbags and backpacks.

The atmosphere on the bus was clouded with fear. Some people trembled, and some could barely breathe.

One of the policemen picked up an Afghan leather fur coat from the overhead rack and demanded to know who it belonged to. Nobody claimed it. He marched up and down the aisle interrogating the passengers and still no one admitted to owning it.

Smuggling drugs in this type of bulky coat was common and the inspectors examined them closely. Perhaps they felt something suspicious sewn in the lining. The coat was stored above two young hippie-like Yugoslav boys and the police accused them of owning the coat. They denied the accusation, panicking and yelling, "No, no!" but the officers grabbed them and violently forced them off the bus.

I held my breath and thought grateful thoughts about the hash that went up in smoke.

We sat frozen, silent in our seats as we watched the two boys leave the bus, yelling, screaming, struggling. I watched from my window as the boys were dragged into the custom office. After five minutes, three men with rifles led them behind the building. Two gunshots were heard.

On the bus, hearts were pounding; most of us were horrified. Some wept, some prayed. A few whispered, "They deserved it." The bus driver confirmed that they were killed because they had tried to smuggle narcotics into the country. It was a major crime in Iran. Their bags were removed from the bus and within a few minutes our journey continued. No one said a word.

Mashhad, Iran

When we arrived at the border town of Mashhad, everyone collected their bags and quickly headed in different directions. I had very little money and needed to sell my ring as soon as possible. I walked into a little near-by jewelry shop and was disappointed when the owner showed no interest. He told me Tehran would be a better place to sell the ring, because it was famous for its jewelry market. With the shopkeeper's advice, I grudgingly went on my way. However, I didn't know how I was going to get to Tehran without money.

My only option was to hitchhike. I had never hitchhiked before and I hesitated as I walked to the highway. I gallantly waved my thumb in the air, smiled and expected a car to stop at any moment. That didn't happen. Many cars whipped by, leaving me extremely frustrated. Eventually, a car did stop and without incident, the driver dropped me off in the center of Tehran.

David, who had lent me the bus money, recommended staying at the Hotel Amir Khabir. Without too much trouble I found the hotel, went to the manager, and asked,

"How much does a room cost for the night?"

"Five dollars per night," he said.

"Could I pay at time of check out?" I asked apprehensively.

"Fine with me," he smiled, "No problem."

Relieved, I checked into my room and took a long-needed shower. Clean, refreshed, and ready to sell my beautiful ring, I headed for the jewelry market. I was excited to think about all the money I would have. I visited four or five jewelry shops and the best offer I got was forty-four dollars. That didn't seem right. I had to get a better price.

In the evening, I sat in the lobby and started talking with a Pakistani carpet dealer who came to Tehran often for business.

"Are you familiar with the jewelry market, at all? I inquired. "I have a ring that I want to sell, and the best offer so far has been forty-four dollars."

The man examined the ring carefully. "I think I can get you a better deal. I'll take it with me now and be back in a few hours." I gave it to him, and he set off.

Eleven o'clock that evening, he returned.

"Well, what did you get for the ring?" I asked anxiously.

"All I could get was nine dollars," he replied. "That's the best I could do."

"What? Why did you accept nine dollars when the best offer had been forty-four dollars?" I was furious. "Go back and get more money or I want my ring back!"

The next day the carpet dealer went back to the market and returned with another nine dollars.

"I could not get the ring back, but I got another nine dollars. Sorry," he said. He handed me the money and walked away.

I wanted to yell and scream at this thief, but I swallowed my anger. I had been taken advantage of by a skilled con-artist and there was nothing I could do about it now. An expensive lesson learned.

At least, I had enough money to pay for my lodging and to send a telegram to my sister, Kusum, in London.

I AM IN IRAN...ON MY WAY TO MUNICH - NEED MONEY - SEND TO AMERICAN EXPRESS BANKING SERVICE - ISTANBUL - WILL PICK IT UP THERE - PRADEEP

After paying for the room, telegram and food, I had ten dollars left.

Before leaving the hotel, I asked the receptionist the best way to get to Izmit, Turkey. She suggested I take a train out of Tehran and continue over the mountain range by bus to the Turkish border.

Turkey and Greece

I HAD JUST ENOUGH MONEY for transportation and a Turkish transient visa. I experienced no difficulties crossing the border and hitched a ride with a truck driver who was driving to Ankara. Before the driver let me off at the train station, he generously gave me some Turkish lire, as well as a blanket and a jacket. With warmth and money in my pocket, I spent a comfortable night at the train station sleeping on a bench. Grateful.

Next morning, I hitched a ride to Istanbul and was dropped off in Sultanahmet.

After wondering around the area for a while, I stumbled upon a little restaurant called the Gangoor Pudding Shop. It was a meeting place for young people, especially young travelers from different countries. Everyone was welcomed, food was inexpensive and sometimes free. I mingled with a group of hippies who invited me to stay at their commune for a couple of nights. Their house was crowded but I found an empty spot on the floor in one of the rooms and claimed it as mine. Here, I slept soundly through the night.

In the morning, I set out to find the American Express

Bank where my sister, hopefully, had sent me money. It was located in Taksim Square, on the European side of Istanbul. I took a ferry across the beautiful blue, busy waters of the Golden Horn, an estuary separating the old and new Istanbul. Taksim Square was crowded and busy, but I was able to locate the bank. I was told the money had not yet arrived.

For two weeks, I traveled back and forth on the ferry and still the money had not come. I figured my sister either didn't have the money or she hadn't received the telegram. It was time to leave Istanbul and continue on my journey north. There were two routes I could take, one was through Bulgaria, a shorter route, but as a Communist country, possibly more difficult to navigate, or through Greece, a longer route, but simpler. I chose Greece, through Thessaloniki.

Hitchhiking became a routine in my nomadic life. Sticking my thumb out was as natural as a hummingbird drinking nectar from a flower. When leaving Istanbul, I didn't have to wait long before a truck stopped. The driver said he wasn't going all the way to Thessaloniki but could drop me off in a town an hour away. It was a small town and as I looked around, I noticed a big sign in front of a hospital which read, "BLOOD DONATIONS NEEDED buying and selling." What luck! I immediately marched into the hospital.

"How much money would I get for donating blood?" I asked.

"Anywhere from fifteen to fifty dollars," the nurse replied.

I signed up. The nurse filled one vial with my blood and said it was worth twenty-two dollars. "Could you draw more blood?" I asked, almost begging.

"It would be risky, because you don't have any more extra blood!" she laughed.

Having money made everything seem easier. I felt more secure and relaxed. I hitched a ride to Thessaloniki and then another ride to a town near the Yugoslavian border. I walked into the customs house, showed my passport and vaccination papers, and proceeded to fill out a questionnaire for my transient visa. *How are you going to travel in Yugoslavia? How much money do you have?* These were two of many questions asked.

Hitchhiking in Yugoslavia was forbidden, and a minimum of two hundred dollars was mandatory in order to enter the country. I had planned on hitchhiking and had less than twenty dollars. I was refused entry.

The immigration officer couldn't help me but suggested that if I obtained a recommendation from a high Greek Police Official describing my need to pass through Yugoslavia to reach Germany, I might get my visa.

It was worth a try, so I hitched a ride back to Thessaloniki. I found the police station and talked with the Chief of Police, explained my situation and emphasized the fact that I want to get to Germany and simply pass through Yugoslavia. He was sympathetic and wrote an impressive full-page letter expressing his concern saying, "I expect full cooperation from the Yugoslav authorities to issue this young man a transient visa, in order for him to continue his travels to Germany."

With letter in hand and regained confidence, I hitched back to the custom house and handed the letter to the immigration officer. He immediately asked for my passport, opened it and stamped "TWO YEARS, NO ENTRY." I was aghast!

I didn't know what to do. This was all wrong. I kept reading the first page of my passport:

THESE ARE TO REQUEST AND
REQUIRE IN THE NAME OF THE
REPUBLIC OF INDIA ALL THOSE
TO WHOM IT MAY CONCERN: TO
ALLOW THE BEARER TO PASS FREELY
WITHOUT LETTER OR HINDRANCE,
TO AFFORD HIM OR HER EVERY
ASSISTANCE AND PROTECTION OF
WHICH HE OR SHE MAY STAND IN
NEED.
BY ORDER OF THE PRESIDENT
OF THE REPUBLIC OF INDIA

I pondered over these words for a long time and gathered the courage to go back again to the custom house and ask to talk with the person in charge. My request was granted. I greeted him respectfully and asked him why my passport had been stamped 'Two Years No Entry'?

Before he could answer, I continued to say, "I am on my way to Munich with no intention of staying in Yugoslavia. I understand the International Law: no one can block anyone's way. Here, at this border, my way to Germany is blocked. I respectfully request that you move your country, or you let me pass." The officer scratched his head, probably in disbelief that I had the audacity to speak out like this, but he paused and took a moment to think about it. I held my breath. He took my passport and re-stamped it:

PERMISSION GRANTED TO CROSS
COUNTRY WITHIN 24 HOURS

I thanked him, and with a big smile on my face and a lilt in my step, I left the room. I now had to confront my other obstacles: the ride and the money.

My plan was to get a ride and find someone who would lend me the two hundred dollars, which I would return as soon as we crossed into Yugoslavia. I walked out to the road where the cars were driving toward the border and stuck out my thumb. A white French Citron stopped and the driver, a robust, jolly overweight gentleman offered me a ride. I hopped in the back seat with two teenagers, who greeted me in English. The driver and his wife didn't speak English, so the children translated for us. The father explained that they were from Switzerland and were on their way to Yugoslavia for a vacation and I explained my predicament. He said he only had traveler's checks and couldn't give me two hundred dollars in cash, but he would be willing to drive me across the border and cover my cost. I was very grateful and settled in nicely with this cheerful family.

The border officials checked all the passports, visas and the money, and then questioned my presence in the car. The Swiss driver, in a loud, authoritative manner, reassured the official, "I am taking care of this young man's financial needs and plan on driving him all the way to Germany." Of course, the family had no intention of driving me that far, and the father expressed no guilt in deceiving the authorities to help me out. With that said, the car and its occupants were allowed to pass.

Yugoslavia

THE SWISS FAMILY DROPPED me off twenty miles from the border in a little town called Skopje. I had no idea what I was going to do, but walking in one direction was a good start. I eventually came upon a park. I noticed a young man sitting on a bench and sat next to him. He was smoking a joint.

"You smoke?" he asked in broken English. I smiled and nodded.

He handed me the joint inquiring, "Are you from India?"

"Yes," I said as I inhaled the sweet smoke.

"Wow, I feel honored," he said taking the joint from me. "You are probably the first Indian to visit Skopje. My name is Dujan, by the way."

"Nice to meet you, my name is Pradeep Parashar."

Dujan was a handsome young man in his mid-twenties. He wore his brown hair shoulder-length and when he spoke to me, I looked straight into sparkling blue eyes. He had long legs, broad shoulders, and an air of confidence. He was a student at the local university, and after an hour of enjoying each other's stories, he invited me to his house where he lived with other college students. That evening they were having a party and Dujan thought I might enjoy meeting some local people.

By eight o'clock, the house was crowded with Yugoslav college students, all bringing food, drinks and a significant amount of hash. I had no trouble mingling with the revelers. Because I came from an exotic country like India, everyone wanted to talk with me; "What is India like?" "How did you get here?" "Where are you going?" By the end of the night, I had received numerous invitations to breakfasts, lunches and dinners. I felt welcomed and a little overwhelmed with all the attention.

Most of the time, however, I spent talking with a girl named Iskara. I had noticed her moving gracefully through the crowd and when I walked by her, I got a whiff of sweet perfume. Her petite body fit well in the tight pants she wore, and her flowing brown hair hung below her shoulder blades. This combination made her extremely sexy. When she invited me to her home for breakfast the next day, I could not refuse. Her winning smile, big brown eyes, and gorgeous body had me hooked.

The next morning, her parents and several friends greeted me and we sat down to an elaborate feast. Her parents were impressed with my past experiences and maturity. They noticed how their daughter was captivated with me. I noticed, too.

Needless to say, the offers to dine with her continued and I enjoyed many family meals.

Things were going well. Life was comfortable, but after three weeks, I wanted to continue on my journey. I explained to Iskara and her parents that it was time for me to move on to Germany to find work. Iskara's father asked if I could wait a week in order for Iskara to travel with me, because she also wanted to find work in Germany. I agreed.

One evening during the week while eating dinner with them, the father suggested, "Since the two of you will be traveling together, perhaps working together, why not maintain a marriage status?" My eyes must have popped out of my head as I stared at him in shock. When my mind finally settled down, I began to think, and had to admit, "Two would be better than one." This led to serious consideration of the proposition. After a lengthy discussion at the table, I agreed to marry her. Within three days, a wedding and celebration party had been organized. As a gift, Iskara's father bought two, one-way tickets from Skopje to Munich. He gave them to Dujan instructing him to give the tickets to me after the ceremony. A new black suit, well-polished black shoes and a white shirt were laid out for me. The family wanted me to be properly dressed.

On the third day, at eight o'clock in the evening the guests, friends, family and neighbors, arrived. Iskara looked radiant wearing a traditional Yugoslavian wedding dress, colorful and elaborately embroidered. I, in my new clothes, felt handsome, but not quite prepared for what was to take place. The wedding ceremony was a small, simple gathering, thirty to forty people. (Small compared to Hindu weddings where five hundred guests or more are the usual.) We celebrated by dancing to traditional music and eating traditional food. During this festivity, Iskara's beauty captivated many feelings within me, and I acknowledged the choice I had made was a good one.

When the celebration was over and the guests had left, Iskara's mother prepared a spare room in the house for me. That was perplexing. I guessed, a tradition? In the morning,

Dujan surprised me with the train tickets and we headed for the train station. At 3:00 p.m. my bride and I boarded the train to Munich to begin a new life.

Finally, we were alone, free of family and friends. I held her hand and snuggled close as we shared our dreams, expectations and future plans. It was difficult to control the passion I felt toward her.

Around midnight, the train stopped. Yugoslavian officials boarded the train to stamp the departure date on passports. Twenty minutes later, the Austrian officials came by to check the passports and stamp the entry date. All went smoothly.

No problems at the borders and no fiascoes!

We were exhausted and dozed off, not hearing any of the announcements being made by the conductor. Hours passed and the train stopped. This woke Iskara, and she decided to get off the train to buy a magazine. As she was paying the cashier, she saw the train doors close and the train slowly pull away from the platform. I was watching while banging on the window to get her attention. I could see the panic on her face. She ran desperately after the train flailing her arms and screaming for the train to stop, but to no avail. I frantically ran to the conductor in the next car ordering him to stop the train because my wife was left behind. He explained that they were out of the railway circulating area and it was impossible to return the train to the platform. He also mentioned that this was an international train and that no one was allowed to get off for any reason.

"Would she be able to travel on another train with the ticket she already had?" I asked.

"She would need to consult with the supervisor at the railway station for help," he replied.

The conductor was friendly and seemed concern about what happened. He was also curious and asked, "How long have you known each other, and how long have you been married?" I looked down at the floor grinning and said, "We've known each other for one month and have been married for only three days."

The conductor smiled, "I hope the train does not cause your separation or divorce." He thought I didn't seem sad or concerned about my wife and added,

"Go take a walk and perhaps, you will find another wife!"

Actually, I felt very concerned and disturbed by this situation and did not know what to do.

Munich, Germany, April 1971

IT WAS LATE MORNING when the train pulled into Munich. I walked along Schleishemer Strasse, confused and depressed. Again, not knowing where I was going.

I needed to move on with or without Iskara.

I walked as though in a daze attempting to absorb the sights and sounds surrounding me. The sidewalk was lined with trees, and park benches were sparsely filled with men and women sitting alone or with friends. An elderly gentleman, sitting on one of the benches, noticed me and said, "*Guten morgen.*" He introduced himself as Hubert and was curious why I was in Germany. I sat down, introduced myself and plunged into my story. When I was finished, he said "Let's get you some coffee and something to eat. I live two blocks away." We walked to a very nice neighborhood and entered an old brick apartment building. After climbing two flights of stairs, he opened the door to his "*Wohnung*." I faced a room completely cluttered with newspapers, books and boxes filled with papers and magazines. There was not a clear surface anywhere. Hubert was a journalist.

He cleared off a small table, found a chair for me to sit

on and proceeded to make breakfast.

While we ate, I reiterated the fact that I needed to find a job and would be willing to do almost anything. He suggested looking in the old part of Munich where many night clubs lined the streets, and the owners were always hiring foreigners, especially those who spoke many languages. I spoke English, Hindi, Punjab and Urdu. Getting a job should not be a problem. Hubert offered me a place to stay until I found something.

The first thing I had to do was to find out what happened to Iskara. I asked Hubert if I could use his address to send an urgent telegram to her father explaining what happened. I sent the telegram asking Iskara's father to let me know her whereabouts and if she were safe. The next day I received a reply:

IF YOU SEE HER LET US KNOW!

I waited for several days and received no further information. I never heard from the father nor Iskara again.

That evening, I walked to the old section of Munich and happened upon a night club filled with people listening and dancing to loud German style music, a beer hall. I asked around for the manager and through the dim light and cigarette smoke, I found him behind the bar.

"Do you have any jobs available?" I yelled, the room being unbearably noisy.

"How many languages do you speak?" he grunted

"Four languages, English, Hindi, Punjab and Urdu," I screamed.

"OK you have a job. Can you start tonight?"

I nodded, yes.

I leaned over the bar straining my ears to hear what this sleazy man was saying to me. "Good. You work from eight o'clock in the evening to two o'clock in the morning. You're to take the club's business cards, walk up and down the street and hand them to people passing by. Encourage them to come into the club. You get five dollars an hour and free food and beer," he explained in his thick accented English.

I knew finding vegetarian food in a beer hall could be difficult, but I was comforted by the fact I had plenty of beer to drink. For three hours, I walked up and down the street passing out the business cards, but I had no luck in coercing people into the establishment. Discouraged, I walked back into the club. In one of the back rooms, I noticed some women dancing in the nude. I wondered if prostitution went on here as well. I could not support that and with a sorry state of mind, went to the manager and asked if I could quit the job. Looking surprised, he said yes and handed me the fifteen dollars I earned. Before I returned to the apartment, I sat myself down at the bar and drank my well-deserved, free beer.

Hubert was awake writing a news report when I arrived. Disheartened, I explained to him my experience at the club and how uncomfortable I felt. He listened and when I was finished, he thought of another place I might try. It was a well-known bakery called Cafe Hoflinger, not far from his place. The owners hired foreigners and offered free room and board. "It would be good for you, being a vegetarian," he said, as he smiled encouragingly.

The next morning, I felt rested and walked with confidence to the bakery. It occupied an entire block on the corner of Schleishemer Strasse and Schellinger Strasse.

The cafe had three large French windows facing the street and as I walked through the front door, I was overcome by the enticing sweet, buttery aromas. A long counter where coffee, pastries, and other baked goods were served, faced me as I walked in. It took over an entire wall. I could see a large kitchen in the back behind the counter where everything was freshly baked. I asked the woman behind the counter if there were any jobs available. She wasn't busy, so she escorted me to a back office where I stood face to face with the manager, John Hoflinger, Jr.

I explained my situation of needing a job. I think he liked me because I showed sincere enthusiasm and I think I came across as a likable guy. I smiled my winning smile. He told me I could start work the next day. My salary would be four dollars an hour, eight hours a day, and time and a half for over time. The manager called the housekeeper, Heidi, and asked her to show me my sleeping quarters and to give me a tour of the rest of the buildings. She had worked at the bakery for more than twenty years and proudly acknowledged her position.

She was a foot taller than me, big boned, and wore her light brown hair in braids wrapped around her head. Her uniform was a simple button-down blue shirtwaist dress. She was efficient, organized, and went out of her way to explain the routine around the bakery. However, I struggled to keep up with her during the tour and couldn't understand everything she said. With the few English words that she did know, she explained that the owner John Hoflinger Sr. lived with his wife next to the bakery in a two-story flat. The dormitory where I would be staying was in a four-story building where two dozen workers lived. There were a few small apartments set aside for employees with families.

Heidi lived there with her two children, Evi and Rupert.

My room, located on the fourth floor housed six beds: simple, clean, and neat. That night, I sat on my bed reflecting upon the experiences that led me here, thankful and relieved that I had a place I could now call home.

The next morning, at six o'clock, I began work as a Baker's Helper. My responsibilities included washing utensils, filling the sugar and flour bins, delivering baked goods from the kitchen to the cafe, sweeping floors, and keeping the kitchen in order. I worked hard and helped out wherever I could. My fellow workers were so impressed with my high energy, agility, and ingenuity that they started calling me the James Bond of Hoflinger's. In fact, most people couldn't pronounce my name, so everyone simply called me James.

The environment at Hoflinger's suited me: I had responsibility, made friends, and perhaps most important, I was making lots of money.

After one month I had earned enough money to buy a VW bug and soon after got my driver's license. With a car, I had the freedom to explore the city and the countryside and drive wherever I wanted.

A few blocks away from the bakery in an area called Schwabing, was a Burger King. I enjoyed going there for a coffee, sitting in my favorite seat and mingling with people. My main reason for going there, however, was to listen to the piped-in music, especially songs sung by Carol King. My favorite, "It's too late Baby, it's too late…" would blast through the amplifiers almost every day. One day while heading for my seat holding my cup of coffee, I noticed the Pakistani woman who was on the Afghan/Iran bus when the two young Yugoslav boys were shot. She recognized me and beckoned me to join her at her table. I went over, sat down opposite her, and we talked about our present situations in Germany. Eventually, our conversation drifted to that horrible incident on the bus. We sat in silence, recollecting those moments. She looked up at me and whispered, “You remember that coat? She paused, “It belonged to me.”

I looked at her in surprise, “I never expected the coat to be yours. Why didn’t you claim it? Two innocent men were killed!”

“It was too bad, but somebody had to die. If I claimed the coat, I would have died. I panicked. I didn’t know what to do. Now I have to live with the fact that two innocent people were killed because of me. I live with a guilty conscience every day and am uncomfortable with my own Karma.” she choked as she continued, “It’s over and nothing can be done. I have to live with these feelings,” she sadly confessed and bowed her head.

I was lost in my own thoughts and wasn’t sure what to say. It was good to know the truth but what kind of person would do that? Where were her morals? I couldn’t say anything. I stood up, gazed down on her in disgust and left the table.

Life was good. However, I needed to improve my German. I signed up for an evening class at the Goethe Sprechen Schole in downtown Munich and eventually my German got to the point where I could join in and sing a few rowdy drinking songs. The work and dormitory life suited me well, but best of all, was the fact I could pay back the “funeral money” that my parents had given me.

Every morning on my way to work, I walked through the parking lot where the owner and his wife parked their cars.

The owner's wife had a very expensive red Ferrari sports car. Whenever I walked by the fancy automobile and noticed a dirty spot on the shiny exterior, I wiped it off. I thought she might appreciate a clean car.

One evening on my way home from work, I noticed the owner walking toward his car. He was preparing to go to the bowling alley with his friends. He noticed me and asked if I'd like to go with them. The bowling team, a group of boisterous, joyful old men in their seventies and eighties needed someone to keep score and keep the bowling balls in order. He told me there would be food, drinks and extra money for my services.

I had nothing else planned, so I agreed to go along. I guessed they liked the way I kept score and laughed at their jokes, because the group of Bavarian men wanted me to accompany them every week. I was honored. Free food, beer, and tips, which equaled my salary, made it impossible for me to refuse such an offer. It turned out they became dependent upon me and if I did not accompany them, they would not go.

At the bakery, employees relied upon Heidi to keep the rooms supplied with towels, sheets, toilet paper, soap, etc. Her dedication, insistence on cleanliness and on following the "rules of the house" (no swearing, drinking in the rooms, being to work on time, etc.), gave the young employees a sense of security. She was their confidant. Most of us were young and away from our families, so Heidi made herself available for talks, tears, and laughter, while providing comfort when needed.

Heidi took a special liking to me and treated me like a family member. When I first arrived, I wasn't used to getting up early every morning, therefore she would come in the dorm at 6:00 a.m. and gently shake me to wake up. She didn't want me to get in trouble with the boss for being late for work. I eventually adjusted to the routine and got to the kitchen before the bakers arrived.

She worried about my food. I was a vegetarian living in a country that survived on bratwurst, sausage and horse meat. She made sure my plate was filled with vegetables and fruit and that bread, cheese, and beer were always available to fill my hungry stomach. This I was grateful for.

When I first arrived in Munich, Heidi took me sightseeing. A place that intrigued me the most was the Dachau Concentration Camp, twenty-five minutes away from Munich. It was here that Adolf Hitler, in 1933, set up the concentration camp. It existed for twelve years, and during that time over 41,000 people were murdered.

The tragedy of war and the dictator who slaughtered all those innocent people had a deep emotional impact on me. Heidi looked as though she had experienced sorrow relating to the camp but didn't talk about it. I went back there several times during my stay in Munich trying to understand the purpose of this disastrous event.

Most of the people I worked with were from Italy or Yugoslavia and could converse with each other in their native tongues, but there was no one for me to talk with in Hindi. Few spoke a little English.

Three months after my arrival, a Pakistani man named Tahir, joined the Hoflinger crew. Even though he didn't speak Hindi, he spoke Urdu, which was close enough, so we were able to converse with one another. We were the same age and enjoyed going to the bars and coffee shops. We talked for hours about our families, girls, our futures and our dreams.

Despite my new friendship with Tahir, I missed my family. I felt homesick and yearned for my parents and siblings. I wrote to my sister Kusum who lived in London with her husband and two young daughters and invited her to come to Munich. In July, she arrived. It had been two years since we had seen each other, and a warm feeling came over me when I saw her. Here was a family member, who spoke a familiar language, and shared part of my past. I found my Hindi words flowing off my tongue like a raging river, uncontrollable, natural and filled with emotion. Her visit lifted my spirits, renewed my sense of self and supplied me with the confidence to continue pursuing my dream of the travel agency.

Because Heidi did not want me to be homesick, she and her children went out of their way to have me for dinners, take me on day trips, see movies, and go on picnics. In fact, Heidi wanted me to settle down in Munich. She knew Evi would be married at some point and Rupert had plans on moving out of Munich soon. But I had my plans which I had not shared with her.

Working at the bakery, washing dishes and sweeping floors was not my idea of a great future.

One day Heidi, Evi and Rupert invited me to go to a small village called Puffenburg, where Heidi recently purchased a house. They had packed a lunch and wanted to celebrate their new home. While we were enjoying the picnic, Evi took me aside to explain that her mother bought the house with expectations of me moving in with her mother when she retired. Then, I would have a place to call home.

I didn't know what to say when Evi approached me and explained her mother's motive. At the moment, I had no definite plans. I didn't want to disappoint this lovely lady who had done so much for me, so I felt obligated to accept her offer. There I was, secure for the rest of my life, working at Hoflinger's and living with my surrogate mother!

Heidi noticed I didn't have a girlfriend. She took it upon herself to introduce me to several suitable girls. However, it took some time for me to gain the courage to ask anyone out on a date. When I did, I asked a beautiful blonde German girl who worked at the counter in the cafe. She was slightly taller than me and wore her long blond braid down her back which added to her undeniable sex appeal. She was carefree, spoke with a thick accent, but we were comfortable with each other. We ate dinner at a nice restaurant and casually walked through town. As we walked, she often stopped and spoke to a few men and sometimes spoke to them in private. Next day at work, my colleagues told me she was a prostitute. The kitchen staff was amused. I was not and did not attempt another date.

Munich was preparing for the upcoming 1972 summer Olympics and the government declared that all unauthorized immigrants had to leave the city, effective immediately.

I fell into that category. As the Munich authorities viewed my records, they noticed my entry permit had expired. Germany didn't require a visitor's visa from Indian Nationals, so it was easy for me to enter Germany. There were only ENTRY and EXIT stamps, good for six months. A couple of days after my meeting with the immigration authorities, two police officers came to the bakery wanting to see my passport. They wanted to confirm that my entry permit had expired. They also became aware that I had no work permit. The officers took my passport and said they'd return it in the afternoon. Everyone at Hoflinger's was whispering and curious why the police had come to the bakery.

At two o'clock, the police returned explaining I had to come with them to the courthouse. I was dressed in my work clothes and was given permission to go to my room to change my clothes. I passed John Sr. and his wife as I was walking upstairs. They were aware of the government's decision with the unauthorized immigrants and said if I needed help to let them know. They were not aware that my entry permit had expired, nor did they know I had never acquired a work permit. No one had ever asked.

By the time I arrived at the police station and the paperwork was completed, the courthouse had closed. That meant I had to stay overnight in custody until the following morning when the courthouse reopened. After a long uncomfortable night of sleeping on a small narrow cot, I was escorted to the court room. To my surprise, I was greeted by a lawyer that Mr. Hoflinger had sent to help with court proceedings.

The Judge talked to me in German/English and asked if I was aware that my entry permit had expired two days ago and that I was working without a work permit? I quickly had to create a convincing explanation.

"First of all, I miscalculated the dates and secondly, I am working at the bakery to earn money in order to support my research project on World War II."

I looked the judge right in the eye. At this point, the judge proclaimed, "You must address your lawyer and your lawyer will talk to me." I was perplexed at this request but did as I was told. I shifted my body to the left, now facing my lawyer and continued, "I am writing my thesis related to World War II and need to interview one hundred German families who were affected by the war. I need work to support my project and I require more time to finish it."

I didn't realize my lawyer's English was incomprehensible, but he turned to the judge and related my story as best he could. There was a short discussion in the courtroom after which the judge turned to me and said, "I want you to come back tomorrow with the paperwork you have so far on your research." I looked at him, smiled and quickly walked out of the courtroom. My head spun around with thoughts on what to do.

I boarded a bus for Heriti, a big shopping mall in the center of Munich. I bought lots of notebook paper, files, paper clips, staples, and pens. My mind explored various plans, calculating a way to outwit the judge.

I stopped at a bookstore and bought some European history books that covered World War II and continued on to Heidi's where I knew she would let me have a space to work quietly throughout the night.

With the work I had done for Pete Wilkins on his research in India, I had learned how to develop a format for an effective questionnaire. Heidi and Evi were willing to help. They contacted twenty-five people who were willing to be interviewed. The senior men from the bowling alley were more than willing to fill out the forms. It was a lot of work and a very long night, but with the help of my friends, I managed to create an authentic image of a thesis in progress.

The next day, bleary-eyed but well prepared, I presented my research project to the judge. My entrance to the courtroom was comical. I stumbled in, awkwardly lugging two canvas bags filled with files and notes, while balancing several heavy history books under my arms. Clumsily, I spread all the papers out on a long wooden table in front of the judge. I gazed upon my hard work with great satisfaction and stepped back from the table. Smiling, I waited for him to speak. I noticed John and his lawyer standing near-by to support me. That was reassuring.

The judge glanced down at the mass of papers on the table, took a long look at me and said, "I order you to leave Germany tomorrow by 5:00 p.m. However, in order for you to continue your research, you can return to Germany the day after and obtain a work permit." I thanked the judge, gathered my things and left the courthouse.

When back in my room at the bakery, I sank down onto my bed exhausted. "Now what? I need to leave Germany, but where can I go? and do I want to return?"

Later that day, I made up my mind to move to Amsterdam. I had a few friends living there and I could stay with them for a while. I'd have time to organize my thoughts. I said good-by to my fellow co-workers, my friends, and gave my car to an Italian baker.

Saying goodbye to Heidi and the Hoflingers was the most difficult thing to do. I apologized to the owners for any mistakes I had made and thanked them for all their help. They reassured me that if I returned, I would always be welcomed.

Heidi and Evi drove me to the train station. We parted with tears, hugs, and promises of my returning and seeing each other again.

Amsterdam

AMSTERDAM EXPLODED WITH THE spirit of the 70's, pot-smoking, prostitution, and expressive art. Electric music by Led Zeppelin, the Beatles, and the Rolling Stones circulated the club scene. I immersed myself in this culture, feeling a refreshing freedom and a thirst for change. I sought out museums, historic buildings and peaceful gardens. These were the places I could gather my thoughts and make future plans.

"Where do I want to live and set up a travel agency? An English-speaking country would be the best, because I could express myself and be understood. England could be a choice, close to Kusum, but I still have not come to terms with the British "Raj" taking over India for those two hundred years. USA or Canada? Dan was in Chicago, Pete Wilkins and many of the American Peace Corps volunteer friends lived in the US. What the hell, why not go there. I'll call Dan. I'll get a job and save money in order to open my business. USA, it is."

A plan for pursuing my dream was made. While I floated around Amsterdam, my money was dwindling away. I either had to find a job or go back to Germany.

While I was deciding what to do, I heard about a cheap charter flight from Frankfurt to New York City. The German Polizie Sports Club arranged the flight with Atlantic Airlines. The DC 10 was scheduled to leave October 18th.

The timing was perfect. I gathered my belongings and hopped a train to Frankfurt, Germany. I found the ticket office for Atlantic Airlines and bought a seat on the flight to New York City, New York. I took another train to Hamburg where the US Consulate was located and applied for a visitor's visa which was good for three months. When I handed the application form to the woman behind the counter, she looked at my Indian passport and asked, "Why didn't you apply for a visa in India?"

"I hadn't thought about going to America when I was in India." I said. I thought she might be implying that I needed to go back to India to apply for this visa. I quickly added, "I have been staying in Germany and now want to visit America."

An hour later I had an interview with the consular.

"I have rejected three hundred and fifty visitor visa applications today, because the applicants had failed to guarantee their return home before their visas expired. Why should I give you a visa?"

I thought for a moment, smiled and asked hopefully, "Perhaps, you will give visa to No.351?"

The consular shook his head, "NO, no, no, but if you can guarantee that you will return in three months, I will give you a visa."

"Sir, am I permitted to ask you a question?" I asked.

"Yes," he said, relaxing back in his chair, looking amused.

"What guarantee do you have that you will be sitting on

that chair tomorrow?" The consular looked perplexed and asked, "What do you mean?"

"There is no guarantee for the future and if I do not like your country, I will return the next day. If I like your country, I will apply to stay. No one including yourself can guarantee that we will be living tomorrow, and you are asking me to guarantee the next three months?"

When I finished, I noticed he looked off into another room. Apparently, it was his coffee break. He wanted to continue our conversation and beckoned me to join him.

"How did you learn to speak English so well?" he asked

"When I was a teenager in India, I associated with the American Peace Corps Volunteers. They taught me English, I taught them Hindi.

"Amazing!" he exclaimed, "I was in the Peace Corps, too, in Nepal. Perhaps, we knew some of the same people?"

Probably not, but we continued talking and sharing stories of our experiences.

After coffee, we went back to his office and he signed my visa application.

No. 351 got his visa after all!

On my return to Munich, my pockets were empty. I went back to the bakery to speak with John Jr., and I explained I would be leaving Germany in three weeks on a flight to New York. I needed to make some money before my journey and asked him if I could return to work until my departure date. He was pleased to see me and was glad that I had a future plan, but John Sr. was not pleased when he learned that I hadn't had a work permit. The business had been penalized for the first time in eighty years, an embarrassing and disgraceful occurrence. In spite of what happened, John Jr. agreed that for such a short time, I could have my job back. It felt good to work side by side with my friends again and I resumed accompanying the senior men to the bowling alley. They were delighted to have me back, in fact, and started giving me bigger tips in order to support my trip to America.

Heidi, on hearing about me leaving for the United States, was deeply disappointed. Her plan to keep me in Munich had failed. I explained to her, "I was not born to do little jobs forever. In America there will be opportunities available to improve my quality of life and I can start the business I have dreamed of for so many years. I will miss you and will think of you often."

I would have three months to explore the possibilities of opening a travel agency, going to school and, if things went well, get an extension for my stay.

When the three weeks in Munich were up, I had enough money for my trip. With mixed emotions I said goodbye to everyone again. I took a train to Frankfurt, boarded the Atlantic Charter Aircraft, and took off for the USA.

Chicago, Illinois, October, 1971

BECAUSE OF UNFAVORABLE WEATHER, the plane landed in Chicago instead of New York. It would continue its service to New York when the weather conditions improved. Since my ultimate destination was Chicago, I inquired if I could disembark at this stop. The stewardess and captain approved, and I collected my two small suitcases from the aircraft.

I breezed through all the long lines and, once the questions were answered, I was allowed to walk onto American soil. The customs official smiled as he said, "Welcome to the USA!"

It was 4:30 a.m. and I knew it was too early to call my friend, so I walked to the waiting room and sat down.

Dan, my English tutor from the Peace Corp, lived in Hyde Park with his Indian wife and infant child. I hadn't seen him in three years and wanted to call him as soon as possible. In order to make my call I needed to exchange my Deutsche Marks to US dollars, but the banks did not open until 8:00 a.m.

I kept looking at the clock, then looking at the bank

and paced back and forth in front of the telephone booth. Apparently, I appeared stressful to a gentleman standing near-by. He sensed the dilemma and generously gave me enough change, plus some, to make my phone call.

At 6:00 a.m., I called Dan. "Good morning, Dan. This is Pradeep. Hope I didn't wake you, but I couldn't wait any longer to call you."

"OK, I don't mind. Where the hell are you?" He asked excitedly.

"I'm at O'Hare Airport."

"I don't believe it! Sangeeta," he yelled to his wife, "this is Pradeep!"

I could hear over the phone that they were pleased to hear from me. Sangeeta told Dan to give me directions and to come to their home right away.

"Go to the elevated train station near the airport, buy a ticket to 55th Street Station and board the Howard-Jackson elevated train going east. It takes one hour. Get off at 55th Street Station and walk two blocks east. You should see South Everett Street. You have the house number? Number 5524. See you soon dear friend." He said and hung up the phone.

When the banks opened, I changed my money. I found the elevated train, bought my ticket and at the last minute unwittingly boarded the wrong train, unaware that the train was heading west, not east. During the ride I thought I'd see some of Chicago's famous buildings, but the train went underground. I missed the landmarks that I had seen on postcards: The John Hancock Center, Chicago Art Museum, and all the high- rise buildings. When the train came out of the tunnel, I had a glimpse of the ghetto and the slum areas of the city, scenes definitely not shown on postcards.

I got off at 55th Street, also known as Garfield Boulevard and lit a cigarette. I glanced around, feeling exhilarated and happy to be in America. My dream of coming to the United States had come true. I was dressed in my German smoky grey wool suit, enhanced with an emerald green tie, wore fashionable high heeled dark brown shoes and had a camera slung over my shoulder. I felt like a classy world traveler.

As I strolled down the street with my two suitcases, walking back and forth looking for South Everett Street, I realized I might be in the wrong area.

I sat down on a bench on the side of the street to figure out what to do next, when a Chicago Police car stopped in front of me. The police officer signaled, in a friendly manner, for me to come over. I approached the car cautiously. What I viewed was a heavy-set middle age man whose uniform fit quite snugly and who was smoking a huge stogie cigar.

"Where are you going, sir?" the officer asked.

I showed him Dan's address.

"And how will you get there?" he inquired.

"I will walk, sir. I love to walk." I replied

"It's a very long walk," said the officer "and if you do walk, you may be killed in ten minutes."

"What do I do?" I asked in a panic.

"There is a laundromat across the street. Go there and call your friend. Have him pick you up and do not leave the laundromat until he arrives," the officer ordered.

I did what the officer said, and lugged my suitcases across the street as quickly as I could. I called Dan, told him where I was and said, "Hurry! I have nine more minutes to live!" Dan arrived in seven.

We spent hours talking about our time together in Gwalior and what he had done since his return to the United States. I told him my story of how I managed to leave India, my travels to Germany and how I accomplished getting a visa to America. He enjoyed hearing about my adventures and was impressed with my perseverance. During the next few days, he escorted me around Chicago, showing me the sights I had missed upon my arrival. We walked along the streets visiting parks, museums, and restaurants so I could familiarize myself with the city. One day, while exploring on my own, I noticed the Butternut Bread Bakery plant. Since I had worked in a bakery before, I thought I might be able to get employment there. So far, I hadn't looked for a job, so that afternoon I walked in and applied. I spoke with the production manager and explained my past experience at the Hoflinger Bakery in Munich.

Ed Weeks was a tall Texan who spoke with a strong slangy drawl. He was a brawny man and to my surprise had spent time in Germany and spoke a little German, as well. He showed me around the factory, explaining the different products and how they were made. He explained the difference between Butternut Bakery and that of Hoflinger Bakery. "This bakery is a fast production bakery with automatic machines compared to people making the individual product," he said, then added, "Look around and see if any of the jobs interest you."

I observed people working in the different areas of the bakery and knew I could fit in somewhere. There were two things I needed, however, before I could start work: a Medical Exam Clearance Form and a Social Security Number.

The following day I made an appointment with the company doctor, had a physical, and was handed my medical form. I continued on to the Social Security office, filled out an application and without being asked for my passport or for any identification, I was presented a SS#. It seemed as though, the IRS and immigration had little communication with each other. With these two papers in hand, I could start work immediately. Luckily, no one checked to see if I had a work permit.

I was hired as a "floater," a union job connected with the local union #1-A, Bakery and Confectionery Workers Union of America AFL-CIO. My responsibilities involved handling the ovens, mixers, and the steam box for staff members while on their lunch breaks. For three months, I worked hard, working overtime, sixty to seventy hours a week. When I had earned enough, I rented an apartment and bought a car.

Because the company noted that I was competent and enthusiastic, they promoted me to a managerial position. In order for me to take this position I had to pass a six months diploma course from the American Institute of Baking located in Chicago. To my relief the company would pay. However, I worried about not having a work permit, worried that my visa was soon to expire, and realized I could not openly say I had a job.

First thing I had to deal with was my visa. I went to the Immigration Office and asked if I could have an extension. Of course, the interviewer asked why. I explained, "I have seen only a portion of the United States and would like to extend my time here in order to see more of your magnificent country." Somehow, I managed to convince the authorities to grant me another three months.

The idea of a travel agency was never forgotten. I continued to plan and organize my approach to making my business happen. Thoughts of studying business law kept crossing my mind, so I enrolled in a correspondence course in business law and immigration at La Salle University.

The three months flew by and in order for me to stay longer in the country, I would have to change my visitor status to a student status. I would need to be a full-time student in a recognized educational institution. Unfortunately, the correspondence course at La Salle did not count. I applied to the Central YMCA Community College and was accepted, but that was not enough. I had to prove that I was financially stable or had a sponsor who was financially sound. Because I worked illegally, I couldn't show my paychecks. One of my colleagues at Butternut offered to sponsor me, but his salary was insufficient. Needless to say, my student visa was rejected. I had to find a clever solution to this unexpected problem.

US Immigration sent me a notice saying I had to fix my departure date within two weeks or explain why I did not want to leave the country. I started reading as many law books I could pertaining to how to remain in the United States legally.

I found three options: 1. If I were a highly skill professional. I was not. 2. If I were a foreign investor. I was not. 3. If I were married to a US citizen. This was a possibility.

At the Blue Gargoyle Club on the University of Chicago Campus, I tacked up a notice on the bulletin board:

> ANYBODY WHO WANTS TO MAKE $2000
> CALL THIS NUMBER
> MUST BE AN "UNMARRIED" WOMAN

Three women responded.

One of the women seemed to be in need of money more than the others. I chose her and we met for breakfast at the Valois Restaurant in Hyde Park.

An attractive Afro-American woman joined me at the table. Shelly Williams grew up on the south side of Chicago and currently worked as a nurse at the University Medical Center. I explained my situation with the following conditions: 1. I would pay her $125 per week until the $2,000 was paid off. 2. We would go our separate ways after the wedding. 3. After six months, I would file for a divorce covering all costs. She agreed to the terms.

The process of the marriage moved quickly. We met on a Saturday, had a blood test on Sunday and on Monday morning we were married at the Cook County Court Room with Ray, a colleague from the bakery, as a witness. When it was time to slip the ring on her finger, I realized I didn't have one. In the rush, I had forgotten all about a ring. Leaving Shelly alone, Ray and I ran from the court room in search of a ring. At a Woolworth's store nearby, we found a bubble gum machine with rings piled inside. After many tries of shaking and yelling at the machine, along with many pennies lost, a ring rolled out. We ran back to the court room. Breathless, I slipped the plastic, pink ring on Shelly's finger.

We had a good laugh.

Immediately after, we went to the Immigration Office and submitted our legal papers: an application for change of status – visitor to permanent – and our marriage certificate. I was satisfied with how the day went until I was told I had to wait six or more months for my change of status to be approved. That was too long. I could not continue with my plans until I had my Green Card. At the end of the day, as agreed in our contract, Shelly and I went our separate ways.

On October 11, 1972, we were summoned to the Immigration Office for an interview. Only I attended.

"Where is your wife?" Asked the interviewer.

"At home." I said.

"Why did your wife not come with you?"

"I don't know."

"It's important that I talk with both of you."

I thought quickly and explained, "After we were married, she changed her religion to Hindu and in my religion the women should not talk to men. If I see my wife talk to you, a male, I must divorce her. Our religious rights would have been violated."

The interviewer, apparently agonizing over this situation, left the room. After ten minutes he returned and told me to come back at 4:00 p.m. At that time, he handed me an envelope and on the front was printed:

WELCOME TO AMERICA

I was overjoyed. I was admitted as a "Lawful Permanent Resident" into the United States and issued an Immigrant Visa under I-151 (Green Card). I was notified under INS form I-357, by the authority of the Attorney General of the United States, which read: "Welcome to the United States of America. You have now been admitted for Permanent Residence. We hope that you will feel completely at home in our country." I also received an "Alien Registration Certificate" certified by the Commissioner of Immigration and Naturalization Service, United States Department of Justice, which read:

"This is to certify that Parashar, Pradeep Kumar, Registration Number A19 725 165 has been duly registered according to law and was admitted to the United States as an immigrant at Port Chicago on October 11, 1972, class Z-2. Date of birth 04.01.1949, sex – M.

On or about October 21, 1972, I was registered with the United States Army under Draft Laws with the "Selective Service Board" (SSB) under the Universal Military Training program in the city of Chicago and classified under H-3 category. I received a new Social Security Number to pay the U.S. taxes and to receive Social Security Old Age Benefits.

The most important thing I would receive was my Green Card and I was told it would arrive in three days by certified mail. With that card I would have a sense of security and could legally move ahead with my business plans.

During this time, I finished the baking course at the American Institute of Baking. The Institute then sent me to three different states to launch new bakery products. I spent most of my time traveling and didn't have time to think about establishing my travel agency. When the work slowed down, I looked for a location for my business. I found an office space on Monroe Street conveniently located near the Immigration Office.

While attending the YMCA College, I met a young man from Pakistan. I told him how I planned to open a travel agency and he seemed very interested. Salamat drove a cab to earn money for school but he expressed an interest in becoming a "silent partner" and playing a small role in the business. He even offered to give me some financial support. Together, we established the Alien Travel Service.

In order to be accredited, travel agencies had to be approved by the International Air Transport Association. A slew of forms had to be filled out, which we managed to do, and we got approved.

Managing the travel agency and working the night shift at the bakery ultimately put a strain on me. I quit my job at the bakery and focused on the agency, but Salamat spent little time promoting the business or helping in the office as originally agreed. Conflict grew between us and in the summer of 1973, the partnership dissolved. One of his relatives took over the business and I opened the World Ways Travel Company in downtown Chicago in front of De Paul University. I had help from several consultants and outside sale agents which helped my new business thrive.

Every now and then I thought of Carol and Chris. Had it not been for them I probably would not be here in the United States. I remembered them as my clients in that small office in Gwalior and of our travels through India. Now, I sat in my well-established office in Chicago, Illinois in the USA with feelings of immense gratitude.

I didn't have any information on Chris, but I did have Carol's parent's phone number. I dialed the number. Her mother answered and remembering who I was, gave me Carol's home phone number. Carol was delighted and surprised to hear from me. She asked so many questions, so fast that I couldn't say a word. During a pause, I offered to send her a round trip airline ticket from Tucson, Arizona, where she now lived, to Chicago.

A week later, she arrived. As we talked about our past and our present lives, I gave her a tour of the city, the vegetarian restaurants, and of course, my travel agency. She was pleased that despite the many crises, hard work, mishaps and deceptions, my dream had come true.

Chris's name and his whereabouts came up in conversation, but Carol had had no contact with him since their trip. He had called her a few times, but she never replied.

In the beginning of 1974, my wife Shelly, who I had not yet divorced and whom I never lived with, gave birth to a male child. Her parents called me to discuss my relationship with their daughter. Since I now was a successful businessman, and could care for her, her child and their grandchild. Shelly's parents suggested that we take our marriage seriously. If we were not to be a "family unit" I would be liable for child support.

Obviously, this was not my child and I did not agree to the arrangement. To avoid conflict, I gave Shelly a substantial amount of money and said I wanted nothing more to do with her. Months later, I received a summons from the welfare department demanding child support. I disagreed with the claim, stating I was not the father of this child. When I told her I would legally fight her if necessary, she dropped the charge.

I lived on the first floor of an apartment building in Hyde Park, South Chicago. My good friend Jack lived on the third floor and Jack's friend Joe, lived a block away. The three of us shared the love of jazz. We spent many evenings together listening to the collections of artists like Duke Ellington, Miles Davis and John Coltrane.

Joe moved from Indiana where in high school he and

some friends formed a band. He played the guitar and the piano and thought living in Chicago would expose him to the finest music around. When he moved to Hyde Park, he met other musicians and they started having weekly jam sessions. I played percussion.

Joe was an easy-going, soft spoken man who stood about 5'8. He was stocky and wore his unruly dark brown hair shoulder length. A thick dark brown beard covered his face. He worked part time at the US Postal Service and part time driving a cab. Jack was medium built, wore a friendly smile, and spoke with a husky, deep voice. He stood 6'and had straight blonde hair which was cut evenly around his head, ear length. He worked at the University of Chicago. We all enjoyed our jobs, but jazz was what we lived for. Every week we would head for a show to catch a famous jazz musician: places like Jazz Showcase, University of Chicago Music Theater, or the Amphitheater in downtown Chicago.

Jack's job at the chemistry lab gave him access to certain chemicals and apparatus. With his knowledge of chemicals, he learned how to extract the oil, THC (tetra hydrochloride), from the marijuana plant and by using petroleum ether, could make hash oil. A special furnace to boil the ether was set up in his bedroom. This operation had been going on in his apartment for two and a half years. It was enjoyed by friends and Vietnam vets who needed to wean off the heavy drugs they had become addicted to during their stint in the war. Needless to say, Jack's apartment was a popular social gathering place where friends met to smoke hash, drink, and play music

One Friday evening, Jack had a party. It lasted all night and into the wee hours of the morning, at which time everyone left but me. I was too tired to go downstairs to my own apartment and opted to sleep on his couch.

Later that morning, we were woken by a sudden crashing noise. Armed policemen came barging into the apartment, moving furniture, throwing books, searching all the rooms, yelling and calling me "The Mahavishnu" (Great God.) We were ordered to sit in the living room and not to move. We sat dumbfounded.

One of the cops called out, "Look, Harry, I found 100 pounds of marijuana in a large bag!" and proceeded to open every kitchen cabinet, including the refrigerator and all visible drawers. They collected, as evidence, all medicines, chemicals, toothpaste, and any suspicious looking package including a box of Nestle's Cocoa which the police thought was Mexican heroin. After the prolonged destructive search, we were taken into custody. While driving along in the police car we heard a flash news report coming from the car's radio announcing: "Narcotic factory was busted by Chicago police, two leaders of the International Brotherhood Organization were arrested." Even though the apparatus was set up in Jack's small bedroom, the police claimed it was the biggest drug bust ever in Chicago's history!

After several hours of sitting on a wooden bench at the police station, ignored by everyone, we were escorted to a conference hall. The chemical apparatus found in Jack's room had been meticulously placed on a table. Around the table stood police chiefs from several surrounding states to learn about this successful operation.

Jack refused to answer any questions. I agreed, but I honestly didn't know anything about the equipment and how it worked. An officer showed me the Nestle Cocoa and asked, "How much of this could a person take at one time?" Trying to be helpful, I said, "Two tablespoons." The officer looked doubtful and said, "I didn't know a person could ingest that much Mexican heroin all at once." I looked at him in surprise and said, "The powder is Nestle Cocoa, not heroin, and I like two tablespoons in my milk." Needless to say, the policeman was embarrassed and annoyed with my flippant answer.

The next day, the "Great Drug Bust in Chicago" made front page headlines in the Chicago Tribune and the Chicago Sun. Headline affirmed: If the two men were convicted, they would be sentenced to jail for 500 years! Bail bond was set for $500,000 each. My US national immigration status would be jeopardized.

Our friends hustled to collect bail money for us. To our relief, they not only collected enough money for bail, but also enough to pay for a famous Italian lawyer who specialized in drug cases.

The hearing date would be held a month later. The lab report would be examined, and the informer would be questioned. On that day more than one hundred people attended the inquisition, including our friends. The lab report revealed that no intoxicating substances were found in the marijuana. It was considered "dead grass." The hash oil had been extracted.

The defense lawyer asked the prosecutor, "On what grounds did the police enter a private citizen's home?"

"They had an arrest warrant based on a reliable source." replied the prosecutor.

"Who is this reliable informant? And what are the qualifications of an informant?"

The prosecutor cleared his voice and responded, "If

someone of good standing is known to the police for at least six months, he could be an informant." The prosecutor pointed to a young man sitting in the front row, acknowledging him as the informant.

The judge addressed the young man, "Sir, how long have you been in Chicago?"

The young man hesitated and answered nervously, "I moved here three months ago, sir, from Fort Wayne, Indiana to attend the University of Chicago."

The judge, disgusted, declared that the arrest warrant was based on an unreliable source and declared that this was an unnecessary inconvenience for two private citizens.

After the ruling, the case was thrown out and everyone in the court room clapped and cheered, including the judge who declared to the crowd, "Even Queen Victoria smoked marijuana!"

The Italian defense lawyer hired for the court case filed a defamation case against the Chicago police claiming 19 million dollars damage for the two young men. Ignoring the lawyer, the prosecutor asked us if we would agree to settle the matter outside of court, if the judge allowed. The acting police chief and the prosecutor would seal the criminal investigation record permanently if we signed the withdrawal of our claim case. We readily agreed. The greedy Italian lawyer was irate when he learned he'd now be out of a lot of money.

As Jack and I were leaving the courthouse, one of the officer's yelled out, "Hey guys, don't smoke that stuff anymore!"

Jack smiled and said, "No chance now, you have all the equipment!"

During all this distraction, I still operated World Ways Travel and in the fall of 1975 opened another agency called Wings and Wheels International Travel Service. It was also located downtown and handled only corporate business accounts.

After the drug bust, some of my friends felt uncomfortable living in Chicago. It was changing and they chose to move elsewhere. Jack moved to New Jersey and Joe to San Francisco.

I felt abandoned, no more parties, no more jam sessions, no more sneaking out to the speakeasies. The fun was over.

At the end of 1975, an icy blizzard blew in from Lake Michigan and covered the entire city of Chicago with snow. The extreme cold and gale force winds brought much discomfort to everyone, including me. I didn't want to fight the fierce moods of Mother Nature any longer.

The year before, Joe and I had driven out to the Denver area for a Bob Dylan concert. I was drawn to the beauty of the mountains. The people seemed more laid back and the city less chaotic than Chicago.

Denver was centrally located on the map, and if I set up my business there, I could serve the people of the Rocky Mountain Region. More than forty thousand Germans and other Europeans lived in this area and they flew back and forth to their homeland regularly. I believed I could be of great assistance to them with their travel needs. Relocating to Denver seemed like a logical place for me to go.

Denver, Colorado, 1976

I PACKED MY 1959 GREEN Pontiac and drove west on I-80, headed for my new home in Denver, Colorado.

When I first arrived, I met with my friend Ed Weeks. He had been the production manager and my boss at the Butternut Bakery Plant in Chicago before he was transferred to the Denver plant. Right away, he asked if I'd like to work with him at the plant. Because he knew I didn't have a place to live, he offered me a room in his house until I had a chance to find something.

Living with a family was a new experience. There were people to talk to and share meals with, and I could cook vegetarian Indian food for everyone. My hot spicy dishes became a regular item on the Weeks family's dinner table.

I liked working at the factory and my job paid very well, but in my spare time I looked around for an appropriate office space for my future business. I eventually found a suitable first floor rental at 2801 East Colfax Avenue near East High School in the Capitol Hill area. Before I launched into setting up the travel agency, I thought I should know something about marketing strategies. I spent time at the library researching everything I could find on the subject. With this new-found knowledge, I hoped to have a professional and successful business.

Within two months, I had World Ways Travel operating as a registered travel agency. A Grand Opening was held, welcoming managers of major airlines and travel industry professionals. I established many connections and built a good clientele; not just in Colorado but in several of the surrounding states, Wyoming, Montana, and Utah, to name a few.

A month later I moved out of Ed's house to an apartment near Capitol Hill, left Butternut Bakery, and found another location for my business. The new office space at 4522 East Colfax Avenue was on the ground floor, bigger, more attractive, and more accessible to the general public.

I often rode my bicycle through City Park. On one of these occasions, I heard someone yell out, "Ram Ram ji" in Hindi. I looked around and saw a young man, "How do you know that?' I asked. He explained that he had just returned from India. Scout worked in the park as a gardener and had often seen me riding my bicycle through the park. He thought it would be fun to say the few Hindi words that he had learned. We went out for a coffee and I shared my story of how I came to the United States and opened a travel agency. Scout, looking for a change, expressed an interest in working with me.

We met several times to discuss the possibility. I felt it was a good match. We had many things in common: He was well traveled, understood tourism and the needs of the traveler, had a good sense of humor, and enjoyed sharing his traveling experiences.

I placed him in charge of marketing and public relations. The agency ran smoothly, and life was good, until April 18, 1978.

My father had died suddenly, and I was needed at home in India. Immediately.

His death was a shock and filled me with great sadness. He was only fifty seven years old. I wrote to him often and shared my dreams and hopes with him. In my last letter, I told him I'd be home in May.

The plane ride to New Delhi was a blur. When I arrived my family greeted me with hugs and tears, but I shed no tears. I could feel nothing, eat nothing, and showed no emotion.

What happened was all I wanted to know.

"There was an accident on a bus." My brother, Rakesh, explained. "Our father had attended a conference being held by Indira Gandhi in Indore. When the conference was over, he boarded the Night Pullman Bus, operated by MP State Government, along with other attendees from the Delhi area. During the trip, he was found dead in his seat."

I wanted to see where this happened, so my brothers and I drove three hours to the location where the police had dragged the body from the bus. We stood there quietly and then walked over to the police station to review the Accident and Medical Reports. The Accident Report stated that my father had had liquor on him and that he had been sitting three seats behind the bus driver. Apparently my father fell asleep with his head outside the window. The police believed that a truck carrying luggage secured with cords which had hooks on the ends, passed too close to the bus and struck his head. He would have died quickly. The other passengers noticed a stream of blood on the floor and yelled for the bus driver to stop.

We were not satisfied with the report and asked to speak with the Police Chief.

"First of all," we said, "our father never drank liquor, ever! Secondly, our father, being a railroad man, would never have put his head out the window. He was well trained and aware of the safety rules. Thirdly, he was not in his assigned seat (normally the seats on buses and trains in India are not transferable), and fourthly, why did the hook hit our father's head but there appeared to be no damage to the outside mirror of the bus? Where are the witnesses? This was no accident. Someone killed our father and we need answers."

We learned that during the meeting in Indore, it was announced that Hari Kumar Parashar would be in charge of the Gwalior Division of the Congress Party. In the morning after the meeting, he boarded a government bus with sixty different caste members. Many on the bus were unhappy that this new congressman was elected. Many did not agree with Mr. Parashar nor with Indira Gandhi. Anger spread within the group. When they stopped for dinner, many of the men drank heavily and brought a bottle of liquor aboard the bus.

Our father's head was smashed from an outside source and liquor was found on his body, yet he was not a drinker. There were too many unanswered questions and we believed that he had been murdered.

Indira Gandhi relied on my father. He had good relationships with politicians of the Congress Party, he was effective with the administrators who managed the bureaucrats and he possessed a deep understanding of all sections of India.

Mrs. Gandhi wanted an advisor who could guide her in policy matters and help maintain stability in the Congress Party. She trusted him and declared him Acting President of Chambal Region. A region which covers the states of central India, Madhya Pradesh, Uttar Pradesh and Rajasthan. They both had great visions for their country.

After my father's cremation, everyone in the family bathed and the house was purified respecting traditional rituals. I stayed with my family for the traditional thirteen days of mourning – *shraddha*. (On the thirteenth day a traditional food is served for Brahmins and outside guests. Hindus believe in reincarnation and that they will be reborn into a future that is based on their past thoughts and actions. It is discouraged to lament too much because the deceased soul must be released to the new world with joy and celebration.)

I flew back to Denver, immersing myself in my work. I began organizing the summer charter flights to London and Frankfurt. I hired several sales and marketing professionals to help expand the business from coast to coast and associated with other business entrepreneurs to learn more about staff management.

My mantras were "Hire the attitude and train the skill. Bad attitude rarely changes to good."

I felt I had hired well and that my staff could be trusted. I hired a manager, Max, experienced in Qantas Australian Airline management; an accountant, Greg, and Scout remained manager of sales. The working environment was pleasant, we worked well together, and the business ran smoothly.

World Ways Travel not only sold airline tickets, but also

organized tours and offered special discounts to US military service personnel. My ultimate goal was to be a specialist in European charter flight operations.

At this time, the Greyhound Bus Company was selling used buses at a reasonable discount rate. I decided to order two with the intention of using them for overland journeys from Munich to Gwalior via New Delhi and Agra. To implement this plan, I would have the buses shipped to Frankfurt, Germany. Once they arrived the plan was to open a new travel office in Frankfurt. The new business would be called BUS STOP TOURS.

My life consisted of bookings, phone calls, answering questions and sorting papers; everything had to do with work. All my friends had relationships, I had none. I went to the Krishna Temple, socialized with a few friends but it wasn't enough. I wanted to have a family at some point, but hadn't found anyone I'd want to spend my life with.

I kept in contact with Joe, my friend from Chicago, who now lived in San Francisco and we had talked about taking a trip across the US on Amtrak. This would give me a chance to relax and regroup. We had talked about meeting in San Francisco to finalize the trip.

In the beginning of December, I gave him a call. Joe's roommate answered.

Her name was Jane.

PART TWO ❋ JANE

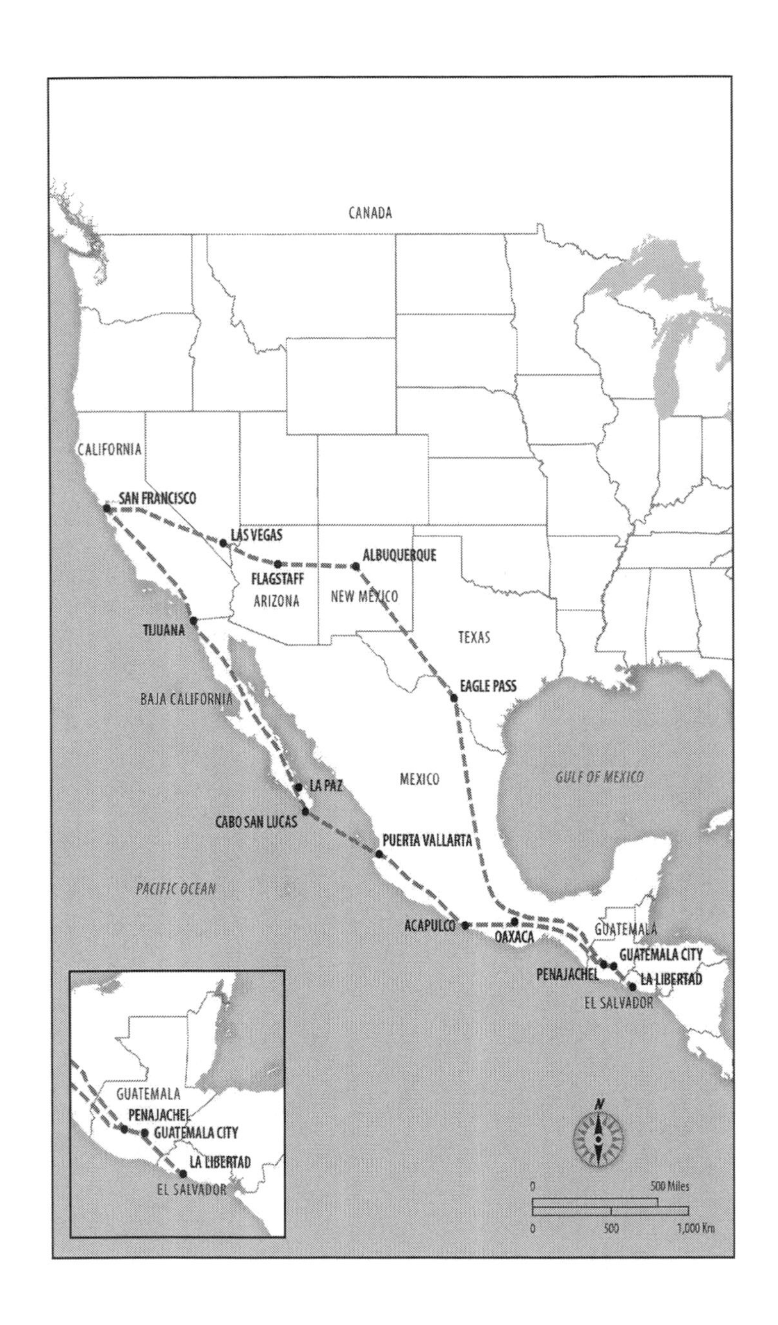
CANADA
CALIFORNIA
SAN FRANCISCO
LAS VEGAS
FLAGSTAFF
ALBUQUERQUE
ARIZONA
NEW MEXICO
TEXAS
TIJUANA
BAJA CALIFORNIA
EAGLE PASS
MEXICO
GULF OF MEXICO
LA PAZ
CABO SAN LUCAS
PUERTA VALLARTA
PACIFIC OCEAN
ACAPULCO
OAXACA
GUATEMALA
GUATEMALA CITY
PENAJACHEL
LA LIBERTAD
EL SALVADOR
GUATEMALA
PENAJACHEL
GUATEMALA CITY
LA LIBERTAD
EL SALVADOR
N
0
500 Miles
0
500
1,000 Km

Gardner, Massachusetts

GARDNER WAS A FACTORY town well known for its furniture. French-Canadian, Polish, Swedish, Italian and Finnish families immigrated there to work in the factories, including my father's parents who came from Finland.

My mother, Ruth Erikson's parents were from Sweden and her father ran a stone engraving business in Quincy, seventy-two miles east of Gardner. This part of the family were churchgoers – Swedish Lutherans – and I was expected to go to Sunday school every Sunday, wear pretty dresses and sit quietly in church while the pastor preached. When visiting my grandparents in Quincy, my grandfather, dressed in a suit and a stylish fedora, would drive us to their church in his big 1949 black four-door Dodge. The women always sat in the back seat, me sitting in between my mother and grandmother. I felt so small.

When I was born in 1946, my father, Leimo Parhiala, was a lieutenant in the Navy and spent a lot of his time traveling. Many times my mother and my two brothers and

I would move with him. Before we settled in Gardner, he was stationed in Trinidad, a little island off the northeastern coast of Venezuela.

Mom, with three little blonde-haired kids in tow, sailed off to meet him. We lived in the capital city of Port-of-Spain in a big house with a wrap-around porch surrounded by palm trees. We had a maid named Ruby and she had black skin. I'd never seen anyone with black skin before, but it seemed to be the norm on the island. We lived with scorpions, tarantulas, and snakes, and Ruby kept us safe … but my mother was terrified! After a year, we moved back to the States and by the time I was eight we had settled down in Gardner.

We lived on seven acres of land with apple trees, chickens, and a pig. Fields and farms surrounded us with stone walls separating the properties. I listened to my father speak Finnish to his family and my mother speak Swedish to hers, and they spoke English to us and to each other.

One thing that Finns desired the most was their sauna, a steam bath. In fact, a community sauna was built in the middle of our town. My grandfather built our house and needless to say, he built a little sauna for the family in the back yard. Ours was a 10x12 building divided into two rooms. One room had a fireplace and a wall with hooks where you hung your clothes. The other room had two tiered benches and two wooden barrels, one barrel for stones and one for water. The heat from the stove pipe of the fireplace would heat the stones and when water was thrown on the stones, it would create steam. It was especially invigorating in the winter when you'd be sweating and could run out into the cold and/or jump into the snow! It seemed however, that my parents had more fun sitting in the sauna than us kids.

My childhood was easy and fun. I belonged to a Brownie Troupe, went to birthday parties, climbed trees, biked with the boys up the street. And then one day, things changed.

I was ten years old. It was February, 1957. My brother Paul and I were listening to Harry Belafonte's famous "Jamaica Farewell" on the record player. We were dancing and singing along when my little brother Billy came running up the stairs yelling, "Daddy's dead, Daddy's dead!"

"Don't say things like that," I said laughing.

"Mommy's crying!"

We turned the music off and ran downstairs, the telegram was lying on the kitchen table, my mother sobbing in the arms of our neighbor.

Leimo Parhiala, 44 years old, had been working in Turkey for the CIA. He and his housemate took a short time off to ski in Austria. We were told that my father did not come down for breakfast. Concerned, his roommate and the manager knocked on the door of his room several times and he did not answer. The manager fetched his key and opened the door finding my father dead in his bed. My mother was told he had died from a heart attack. Because he worked for the government with the secret service, our family could be told nothing more. Were there problems in Turkey and threats being put upon the secret service agents? Did he really die of natural causes or was he murdered? We did not know. My father was a scholar. He studied at Yale and Syracuse, taught at MIT, and spoke five languages. He fought in WW II and in Korea. He served his country well and we grieved. My mother and her three kids struggled for normalcy.

I wanted my mother to be happy and she seemed to be just that when she married Ralph Hendrickson a year later. He grew up in a Finnish family and he, like my father, spoke fluent Finnish. He worked in Fitchburg, a nearby town, as a draftsman. He enjoyed smoking cigarettes but when my mother told him we had no ashtrays, he stopped. He was a good man.

I had a hard time accepting him, though. I was moody and rude and ignored him. I rebelled. He knew it was difficult to have a stranger come into the house and just let me be. After a year, I realized he was here to stay and felt more comfortable with him being part of our family.

In high school I joined the drama club, marched in the band as a majorette and took ballet lessons. I kept active because I didn't do well in my studies and had a complex about my low grades. My friends were smart, heading to prestigious colleges and universities while I was destined to go to a state college, not knowing what I wanted to do with the rest of my life. I wished for something exciting, something to inspire me.

The years passed with family trips, high school graduations and future dreams. The country grieved with the assassination of President Kennedy, and the nation demonstrated against the Vietnam War. The Beatles and the hippie era took over the world.

Newton, Massachusetts, 1966

I SCRAMBLED INTO MY SCRUBS and raced through the swinging doors to the O.R. where my fellow nursing students were observing a birth. Late again. My supervisors scowled. During my first year of nursing school, classmates had nicknamed me "Calamity Jane." Not a good sign.

In fact my teachers were never pleased with me. My hands shook when I gave a patient an injection, I winced at large amounts of blood, cried when I left the children's hospital and at the VA Hospital was aghast at the injuries the soldiers had endured during the Vietnam war and wept for their pain and suffering.

I dropped out of the nursing program but continued my academic studies. My lab partner in micro-biology class was a girl from Sweden. Ulla worked as an au pair for a family who happened to live on the same street as I did in West Newton.

Because my grandmother on my mother's side came from Sweden, I wanted to know everything about Ulla, her country, her trip, her family, what town she lived in, etc. Needless to say, we became good friends.

After receiving an Associate Degree in "nothing," I had no idea what I was going to do and was, once again, uncertain about my future. Ulla suggested I join her in Sweden at the end of the summer and stay with her and her mother for a couple of months to think things over.

I left Newton, and my nursing career and moved back home to live with my parents until I had a plan. I thought about Ulla's offer and decided to join her in Sweden. In order to go, of course, I needed to earn some money. I got a job as a nurse's aide at the local State Hospital and saved every penny in order to pay for my trip. I found that the airfare was just as expensive as a cruise ship, $550. The thought of an ocean voyage excited me … the open water of the Atlantic, rolling seas, a handsome captain in uniform and dressing up for dinner… it certainly would be more of an adventure than sitting on a plane. Seasickness never crossed my mind!

In September of 1968 I stood at the Port Authority in New York City with my mother and stepfather beside me gaping up at the massive ship I was about to board. Enormous…at least two football fields long!

I'd be traveling alone for the first time in my life, sailing on the *Sagafjord*, a Norwegian ocean liner, to Oslo, Norway, then taking a train to Stockholm, Sweden. Nineteen years old and I would be in the middle of the Atlantic Ocean for nine days without knowing a soul. I was terrified.

The Port Authority was filled with hustle and bustle, people of all nationalities racing to find their place of departure, lugging suitcases, tugging at their children. Luggage and crates took over the space on the docks. Ships, large and small, tied onto pilings. Chaos was everywhere. I held my mother and stepfather tightly, tears in my eyes, as I said good-by. They let me go and I could tell they were trying to be as brave as I was.

My heart raced, my knees literally shook as I stumbled up the gang plank onto the ship's deck carrying my suitcase. For the past few months I had been confident, even a little cocky when talking about my trip to Sweden … "a piece of cake," I boasted.

But now, as I waved goodbye to my parents, I wasn't so sure.

As the ship slipped silently away from the harbor, I waved farewell to the Statue of Liberty, farewell to my friends and family, and to the town I had no future in. I said good-by to my old self and hoped to develop into a new me. The wind blew against my face, cool and determined. I closed my eyes and breathed deeply, for courage.

The trip across the Atlantic proved to be exhilarating: three meals a day, dinner with the captain, dancing, talking with the "older people," running laps around the deck. But the most fun was in the evenings when the young people, I believe there were only four of us, would sneak down to the bottom of the ship where the crew lived. Here we would come together with strangers our own age to drink, listen to records, and dance. (Songs by the Beatles and the Rolling Stones were most popular.) No one, it seemed, spoke the same language. It was hilarious … French, Greek, Italian, Spanish, Turkish, English spilling into each other … no matter what our color of skin or religion or language, we lived for the moment and for pure fun.

Once I reached Oslo, I boarded a train to Stockholm where I was to meet my friend Ulla. While passing through the beautiful countries of Norway and Sweden, I thought how lucky I was to have this opportunity and knew it was the right choice.

Sweden, 1968-69

The year I spent in Stockholm, was one of discovery; a new country, a new language, cooking and baking, schnapps, and drinking lots of coffee, new friends. I discovered things about myself: I had stamina, determination and I could get myself anywhere I needed to with confidence; I could take on responsibility and follow through on obligations. I also learned to speak Swedish!

I found a job as an "au pair" with a family and took care of three children. When I had time off, I traveled to Finland and visited relatives in Helsinki. In the winter, I joined a group of students from the University of Stockholm for a ski week in Kitsbuhel, Austria. St. Anton am Arlberg, in Tyrol, was another ski resort located 117 miles from Kitsbuhel and it was there that my father died in 1956. I looked at the mountain range that separated the two ski resorts and remembered that day, the day I learned my father would never come home again.

What I realized during my year abroad was how much I didn't know. The friends I met who were my age spoke three or four languages and their English was impeccable. They knew not only European history, but the history of the USA as well, and I'm sure could name all the States if asked. They knew more about the Grand Canyon than I did. I'd traveled with my family once to Florida and once to

Wisconsin. I knew New England and that was it.

What I learned about myself was that I needed more. I wanted to get my degree in teaching; I wanted to drive across my country and see every state; I wanted to experience new languages and explore different cultures. I had found my new self.

When my visa expired, I sailed across the Atlantic, once again, this time back to the USA with a plan.

In 1971 I graduated from Fitchburg State College with a Special Education Degree in teaching, got a job on Cape Cod, but after a year, decided to leave Massachusetts and drive to California with my friend Kathy. We stopped in Long Beach where Kathy's mother lived. She remained with her mother and I moved in with my older brother, Paul and his family in Huntington Beach. A month later I found a job in Hermosa Beach teaching kindergarten in a private school. So, my life in California began; I had a job that I liked, biked along the beach, played volleyball, had a few lovers, raced Hobie cats, drove to Tijuana and drank tequila in the run-down bars, even learned Spanish. Eventually, I moved to Santa Cruz, then headed north to San Francisco.

For two years, I had lived in this beautiful city. It was 1976. The "flower children" era had slowed down but Haight-Ashbury still had its charm of eclectic and eccentric people…it was the age of the marijuana culture. Everyone smoked weed and a lot of people grew it even though it was illegal. I seldom smoked because I didn't want to lose control. I wanted to be clear-headed and I didn't like the taste.

I enjoyed my teaching job, my colleagues and the school I worked in. All was fine until the spring of 1978 when I was told I didn't have a job come September.

San Francisco, 1978

KIRK, WHO I ROOMED with, and I had been teachers at the Patrick Henry Elementary School in San Francisco, but because of low district enrollment some schools were closed. Patrick Henry was one of them. Many of the teachers were left without a teaching position. Kirk and I fell into that category. Unemployed.

My friend Linda was also unemployed, so we decided to take a two-week trip to Baja California, camp in Cabo St. Lucas and return home. However, since neither one of us had been to Puerta Vallarta, Mexico, and there happened to be an overnight ferry headed for the Mexican town, we decided to continue on with our travels.

On the ferry we met two young, tanned, blond-haired Californian men who were headed for El Salvador to shoot a video on "yoga and surfing." They were members of a spiritual organization who followed Yogananda and practiced Kriya yoga. They said they could use some help with the project and asked if we'd like to join them. I had never been to El Salvador and they seemed like nice guys, so I said, "Sure, I'll go!"

Linda shrugged, saying, "No thanks, I'm needed back home."

John, Curt, and I loaded my gear into their well-equipped truck and drove south to Acapulco where they did some surfing. Then we traveled through the jungles of Guatemala, and finally settled in the little village of La Libertad on the coast of El Salvador.

For two months I spent my time lugging a video camera on my shoulders, standing on sandy beaches photographing my friends in different yoga configurations on their surfboards and watching for the perfect wave.

The atmosphere in the village was serene, filled with meditating and chanting from the followers of Yogananda.

Meanwhile, there were rumors of a revolution going on in Nicaragua, and when we ventured into San Salvador, the capital of El Salvador, we noticed soldiers standing on every corner carrying rifles on their backs. I became nervous about the political situation in Central America, and after fighting off cockroaches, sitting on a scorpion (an excruciatingly painful experience which the thought of dying did not help), and discovering most everyone around me was high on cocaine, I decided it was time to go home.

However, being kicked off the bus at the Guatemalan border was not in the plan. As I clumsily stumbled off the bus, lugging all my bags, embarrassed beyond description, I carefully looked around: no other travelers, no cafes, nothing but a little wooden building surrounded by trees and two border guards. The bus pulled away leaving a cloud of black exhaust in my face. I was alone. It was silent. No one in La Libertad, El Salvador, where I had been hanging out for the past two months, had said anything about needing a visa for Guatemala. I took my bags to the weathered building where the border guards stood.

"Perdon. No tengo visa para Guatemala. Que hago ahora?" I asked.

They told me I must go to a village, five miles away, to get my passport stamped. They allowed me to store my belongings behind their desk and pointed in the direction of the town. Since there were no buses or taxis, I had no choice but to hitch a ride. I had done some hitchhiking on Martha's Vineyard, a small island off the eastern coast of Massachusetts, where I had spent my summers while in college. I hitched another time from Denmark to Sweden. But in Central America? This seemed more than a little risky.

I stood by the road with my thumb out and prayed for my Mayan Goddesses to protect me. Prior to my trip to El Salvador, I treated myself to a session with a psychic reader who also did aura readings. She saw little Mayan Goddesses sitting on my shoulders and said they were my protectors. They would guide me and keep me safe. So far, the little goddesses have served me well.

Within a few minutes, an old truck, loaded with what looked like young fir trees, pulled over. A father and his young son were delivering the trees to a village near where I needed to go, and they gladly gave me a ride. I communicated with them in simple three-word sentences, stumbling along trying to make conversation. My two escorts gave me the impression they understood what I said, smiling and nodding their heads. It was a pleasant ride even though the truck bounced along the bumpy and narrow road. They dropped me off at the edge of town, only a few minutes' walk to the main street. Simple one- story structures lined the street, no sidewalks, just a dirt dusty road.

I walked along looking for something resembling a government building and finally spotted a small official sign on a faded wooden door. No flags flying; nothing inviting about it. The gloomy room inside measured 12'x12', at most, with an old scratched desk and a few rickety chairs lining the wall. The official behind the desk, dressed in a well-worn beige uniform, stared at me with a flat expression. With a swift movement of his hand, he grabbed my passport, stamped it and almost threw it back to me. With no eye contact and no words, he impatiently waved me away. That was it. It took all of two minutes! And now, I had to hitch my way back to the border. When I got out to the street, I noticed a young couple driving by in a convertible. They stopped on the side of the street to talk to some friends and amazingly they spoke in English. I ran up to them and asked, if by any chance, they were headed for the border.

"No, but we'll take you there anyway."

At the border, in my best accent I said, "*muchas gracias*" and gave them gas money. With visa in hand, I could get back on the bus and head for Guatemala City, then catch a bus to the States and make it home for Thanksgiving.

It was not to be that easy.

The border guards had watched over my things. Everything was intact. I thanked them and they smiled. A bus pulled up and confidently I boarded with ticket, visa and all my bags, but as soon as I was on the bus, I was quickly escorted off. The bus driver mumbled something in Span- ish which I didn't understand. When the next bus arrived, I got on and again was escorted off. This time, the bus driver slowly explained in Spanish, that I did not have the right ticket.

The border guards further explained that my ticket was good only for the bus I was originally on and could not be used for any other bus. Why didn't they tell me that before? Meanwhile it was getting late and there were no more buses arriving that day. I certainly had no intention of staying over- night at the border with those border guys! Fear and anxiety swept over me. "I must not panic. I must not panic," was my mantra.

While I frantically thought about what to do, a yellow VW Bug drove up. I watched the car and its driver closely. The fellow driving the car stopped to show his entry papers. He was laughing and joking with the border guards as if he knew them. I had to think quickly. He seemed familiar with the guards, appeared to have a cheerful disposition and was driving a VW Bug. I owned a VW Bug, too. I concluded he must be a nice guy. I knew I was taking a risk, but I was desperate, so I prayed again to my Mayan Goddesses and then dashed to the car. I leaned into the open window of the passenger side. Trying not to look too anxious, I said, "Excuse me, are you going to Guatemala City by any chance?"

With a warm smile, he asked, "You need a ride?"

"Yes," I exclaimed.

"Hop in," he said as he moved his belongings from the passenger seat.

I gathered my bags, threw them in the back seat and climbed in next to "my savior." I showed the guards my pass- port and visa. They smiled. I smiled. My driver smiled. And off we went!

The fellow sitting next to me in the driver's seat was a handsome dark-skinned man in his late-30's. His cheerful friendly manner helped me relax and reassured me that

I had made the right decision. He was a professor at the University of El Salvador headed for Guatemala to play basketball with his college team. He had studied at the University of Guatemala and played in tournaments. The trip was enjoyable and passed quickly. When we reached Guatemala City, he drove me to a hotel where many of his buddies were staying and told them to take good care of me. I was not too sure what that meant but the 6'4"- 6'6" basketball players watched over me like guardian angels until I left two days later.

When it was time for me to leave, they suggested, instead of my going back to California right away, that I take a detour to Penehachel on Lake Attitlan. "You must see this enchanting village before you leave Guatemala." they urged.

So, that's what I did.

"Mario's," a plywood motel, was cheap and a perfect haven for all travelers with little money. The wooden cubicles were furnished with a single bed, a night table, a hook on the door and room enough for a backpack to be placed on the floor. That's all a traveler really needed, just a place to rest one's head. A dollar a night. Couldn't beat that!

Penehachel was a beautiful little village overlooking Lake Attitlan. In the distance you could see the Attitlan Volcano spewing hot red lava. A lot of ex-pats lived there, and travelers visited to relax, hike, enjoy the scenery, and to smoke an occasional joint or two, or more.

I happened to arrive in Penehachel a few days before Thanksgiving, not making it home for mom's turkey dinner. But I did spend the holiday with other travelers sitting in the warm sun eating chicken, rice, beans, corn tortillas and listening to a mariachi band. It was a welcome change from sitting in a living room watching a football game. However, secretly, we all yearned for turkey!

I needed to get back to California for Christmas because my parents were flying out from Massachusetts to celebrate the holiday with my brother in Fremont and I planned on joining them. This I could not miss.

Within a week I had met two women from California who were heading back to Berkeley in a few days. They were buyers for an import/export business and the van was packed with weavings, clothing and other handmade items plus all their gear. They agreed there was enough room for one more person. We re-packed and organized the van, in order for all of us to be comfortable.

On a glorious sunny morning, we left Penehechel and headed for California. We were going to have a lot of time together to share our life's stories. We discovered we had much in common, the love of textiles for one, and surprisingly we resembled each other: the same height, 5'6" and slight build, shoulder length blonde hair and each of us wore granny glasses. We were a perfect team!

We had many adventures on the trip back home, mostly with the VW periodically breaking down, but we made it across the Texas border having only to give up my handspun wool that one of the local weavers had given me. No hassles.

We arrived in San Francisco the first week of December just in time to prepare for the holidays and for me to look for a job.

PART THREE ❁ TWO VOICES EAST & WEST

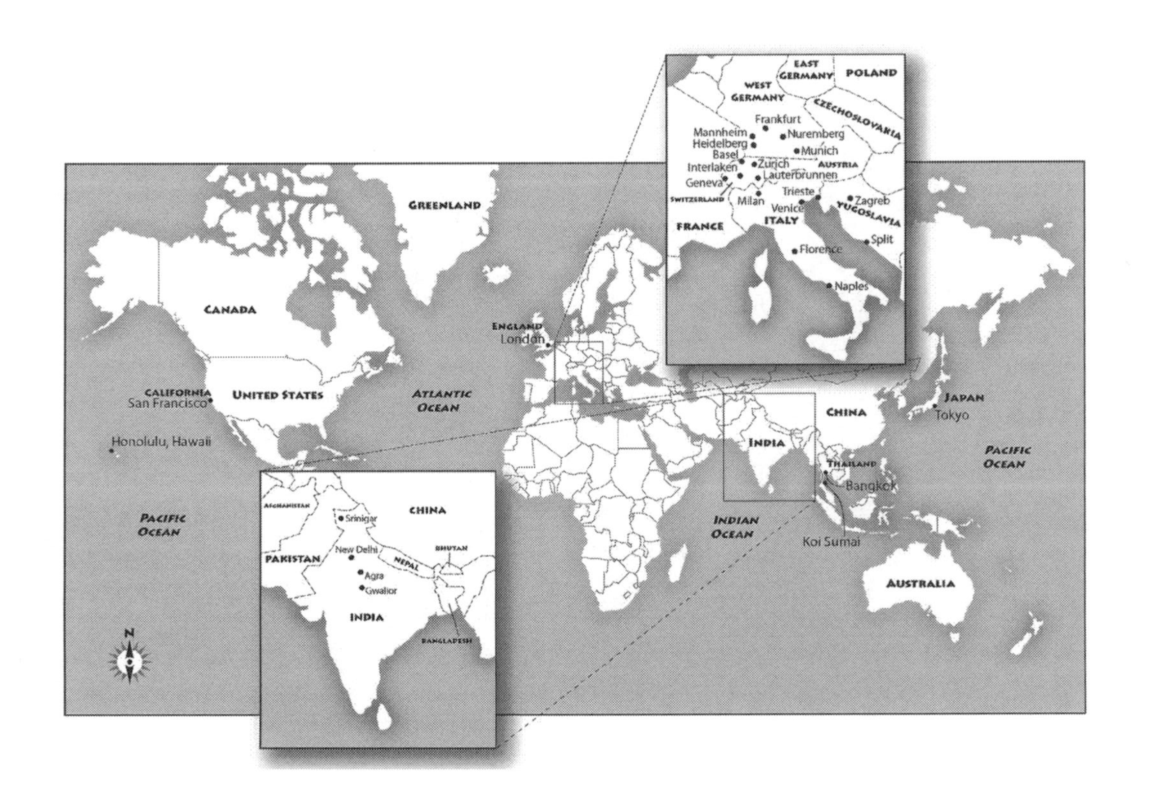
Canada
Greenland
United States
California
San Francisco
Honolulu, Hawaii
Pacific Ocean
Atlantic Ocean
England
London
Indian Ocean
China
India
Thailand
Bangkok
Koi Sumai
Japan
Tokyo
Pacific Ocean
Australia
N
East Germany
Poland
West Germany
Czechoslovakia
Frankfurt
Mannheim
Heidelberg
Nuremberg
Munich
Basel
Zurich
Austria
Interlaken
Lauterbrunnen
Geneva
Trieste
Zagreb
Switzerland
Milan
Venice
Yugoslavia
France
Italy
Split
Florence
Naples
Afghanistan
Srinigar
China
Pakistan
New Delhi
Bhutan
Nepal
Agra
Gwalior
India
Bangladesh

West Meets East ... Jane

I HAD MOVED BACK INTO MY friend Kirk's apartment along with our other roommate, Joe, in Noe Valley where I had lived before. My room was actually a big closet, big enough for a twin-size mattress, a dresser, a chair and lots of hangers.

One large window with lace curtains gave the closet light and a little female flair.

Each morning, while the coffee was perking, either Kirk or I would run down to the bagel shop, bringing home breakfast and a couple of newspapers. We would sit around the kitchen table, sip coffee, eat, talk and search through the help-wanted ads looking for a suitable job.

One morning, a week after my arrival, while sitting in the kitchen shuffling through the newspaper, the telephone rang. I answered the call. It was for Joe. He worked for the Recreation Center for the Handicapped and was active in the music scene in San Francisco, so he was rarely home.

I politely offered to take a message.

It was his friend, Pradeep from Denver, who wanted to get in touch with him to discuss their Amtrak travel plans.

He called several times during that week and each time I answered. Because Joe was not around, Pradeep and I would talk for what seemed like hours.

Pradeep's accent and manner of speaking intrigued me, and every time the phone rang, I hoped he would be at the other end. I learned that he grew up in India, had lived in the USA for almost 10 years and owned his own travel agency. Needless to say, I was impressed. He had a great sense of humor and expressed delight in telling me stories of his travels and dreams. Throughout our conversations, he also expressed a spiritual essence, talking of Karma, Hinduism, God. He activated something within me, filling a need to express myself, to be someone different. I anxiously looked forward to meeting him when he came to visit Joe.

A week before Christmas, he came to the apartment. I felt nervous but, at the same time, excited to finally meet the person I had been forming a relationship with over the tele- phone. When we greeted each other, I found myself instantly attracted to his big warm smile and his natural, agile, comfortable manner.

Pradeep was 30 years old with a slight build, thick soft curly black hair, and a short full well-kept beard. I was intrigued with this young dark-skinned man and when I noticed a twinkle of mischief in his deep brown eyes, I knew I wanted more of him.

We spent the day together exploring Market Street, Fisherman's Wharf, and China Town and eventually ate Japanese food in Japantown. I had lived in San Francisco for two years and had seen these sights many times before, but it felt extra special walking around with Pradeep. And it felt natural when he took my hand as we crossed the busy streets. It also felt natural when reaching the apartment, he gave me a gentle kiss on the cheek. What followed for the rest of the evening felt quite natural too.

Meeting him altered my way of looking at my current situation. I had planned to teach school in San Francisco, live with Kirk and Joe, take dance and art classes, but now, I was obsessed with irrational thoughts. A life with an Indian man ran through my mind and I'd known him for only a month, mainly through telephone conversations.

After his visit, we continued to talk on the telephone almost every day. When he asked if I would like to visit him in Denver, I said "yes," with no hesitation.

Spending time with him and experiencing his world in Denver opened my eyes to new sights, smells and tastes. One night, he took me to an exotic Moroccan restaurant called "*Mataam Fez,*" which was located across the street from his agency.

We entered a dimly lit room filled with low round tables surrounded by cushions on the floor. The decor was ornate, Eastern with colorful cloth billowing from the ceiling. The Moroccan waiter escorted us to a table where we sat on the firm red pillows. Pradeep had eaten there many times before and knew what to expect, but for me, it was a storybook fantasy. Before any food appeared, the waiter presented us with a towel which we placed on our left shoulder. Then the waiter set an urn on the table, asked us to place our hands palm up over it and with an ornate pitcher ceremoniously poured warm lemon water over our hands, to be dried with the towel.

The meal consisted of five courses: first, a lentil soup; second, a medley of spiced vegetables; third, a phyllo dough pie sprinkled with powdered sugar; fourth, the main meal, a thick vegetable baked pie; fifth, fruit served with tea. No utensils appeared on the table; fingers were the only option. Food slipped through my fingers and as it reached my mouth, the sauces dripped onto my chin and hands, making a mess. We laughed hysterically and enjoyed every mouthful.

Pradeep introduced me to the people who worked for him at World Ways Travel and proudly showed me his office on E. Colfax St. This young man from India whom I had known for such a short time continued to fascinate me.

He shared more stories of his youth and his family, of how and why he left India. I listened intently to the philosophy of Hinduism and to his explanation of karma.

Karma, as he was brought up to believe, was made up of three modes of action: intelligence, patience and ignorance.

> 1. **Intelligence** - If action is performed in the mode of intelligence, then the result we obtain is positive; almost 100% guaranteed. In short, we get what we want.
>
> 2. **Patience** - If action is performed in the mode of patience, then the result we obtain is "fruit of activity." It means, if we grow potatoes, we do not get onions.
>
> 3. **Ignorance** - If action is performed in the mode of ignorance, then it results in "blind risk:" gambling, luck, which can irritate, upset, create anxiety and anger.

Indian traditions were extremely different from the traditions I grew up with in Massachusetts. I was raised as a Swedish Lutheran, eating meatballs, herring, *limpa* (sweet rye bread), cardamon coffee bread and strong dark coffee. Even though I was born and raised in the United States, my Swedish-Finnish heritage played an important part in my upbringing. Christmas was the most celebrated, with its Swedish sugar cookies, breads and glögg (a spiced, hot drink), hymns sung in Swedish, *Sankta Lucia*, The Festival of Lights, and big family gatherings. Life centered around the church, Sunday School, Junior Luther League, choir, and of course being a Girl Scout and a Rainbow Girl (an organization for young girls connected with the Masons) was expected.

Pradeep grew up a Hindu, a vegetarian eating *roti*, a flat round bread, curries, *Mattar Pannir* (peas and cheese), drinking *marsala chai* (spicy tea) and *lassis* (a spicy yogurt drink). His life centered around the Krishna Temple with elaborate colorful celebrations such as *Diwali*, Festival of Lights and *Makar Sankranti*, Harvest Festival. But no matter the color of skin, religious background, or way of eating, I felt it made no difference in our growing relationship.

Still unemployed, I had to make a decision about my future. I'd always enjoyed teaching, felt comfortable in the classroom, and loved the challenge of every class. Watching my students engage in learning gave me a great deal of satisfaction, but maybe a change was needed.

Perhaps, I could work in Pradeep's travel agency, he could have me on as an intern. Maybe move to Denver and live with him. What was I thinking? I was fantasizing too fast too soon. Should I stay in San Francisco and continue to look for work or should I risk the unknown and move to Denver to pursue my relationship with Pradeep?

These were questions I was asking myself. Talking with him would be the logical thing to do.

During one of his visits, as we were walking through UC Berkeley Campus, he suddenly turned to me and said, "Why don't we get married?" I was shocked. Time stood still. We just smiled at each other. He waited for an answer.

This is what quickly ran through my mind: I was 32, had never been married. What an adventure this would be. I could travel, be involved in a travel business and be with this exotic man from India. My mother would stop telling her friends that her daughter was an old maid and that she had no hopes of her daughter ever marrying.

Did I say yes out of love? Probably not. Loving someone takes time. Two months was not an appropriate amount of time to get to know and understand someone. I thought of him as a friend, who I thought over time I could love. He was sensitive and attentive. He seemed ambitious and focused. My decision was made.

He probably expected me to say, "Let me think about it." or "Let's sit down and talk about it," or "Wow, thanks. I'll let you know next week." No, no, the impulsive me blurted out, "Yes!"

What was I thinking? I have been known to be spontaneous and unpredictable; fascinated with other cultures and attracted to the eccentric, but this, a marriage? Could we make this work?

I called my mother and told her I was engaged to a man from India. I'm sure she had to sit down!

I neglected to tell her, however, that he had dark skin,

was a Hindu (a what? she would ask) or that he smoked hash. What I did say was that he owned a travel agency, was well respected and had a green card, ("A what? she asked). He was kind, funny and we both loved to travel.

My life was about to change. I had a wedding to plan, and I was happy.

East Meets West . . . Pradeep

ONCE I SETTLED INTO a routine in Denver, I got in touch with Joe. We had discussed taking a trip together. Sometime after our discussion, I tried calling him several times again, but he never seemed to be around. Every time I did call, his roommate, Jane would answer the phone. I found her enjoyable to talk with, so we spent time talking and got to know each other. Finally, I reached Joe and we planned that I should visit him in order to arrange our cross-country trip on Amtrak. By then I'd been talking with Jane for a good two weeks and was looking forward to meeting her.

When I arrived in San Francisco I rented a car from National Car Rental. They gave me a new 1978 red Chevy Camaro z28. It was cool. I was hip, like "a super fly!"

After spending the first couple of days with Joe, I finally had time to talk with Jane. Joe, Kirk, Jane and I were eating breakfast in the kitchen when Joe said he wanted to show me more of San Francisco. Jane had also offered to show me around in her 1968 VW "hippie bug." I explained to Joe that I would like to go with her today. Actually, I wanted to drive my car. I never trusted anyone else's driving and today I wanted to impress this beautiful woman with my flashy car. We spent the day driving around the city in my rented red Chevy. We walked to various sights of interest, talking and laughing. A very pleasant easy day.

I felt some affection for her and wanted to know her better and become closer friends.

It was more an infatuation. Love, the way I see it, requires awe, admiration and respect. It's a man's job to respect women but it's a woman's job to give him something to respect. I believe we are free to choose, but we are not free from the consequences of our choices. I think Jane and I had a discussion regarding these thoughts. Because we discovered we had a lot in common, the love of travel, cooking, and music, we found it easy to be with each other.

After dinner at a Buddhist restaurant in Japantown we took a walk. I remember telling her "No matter how perfect someone else's life looks like from the outside we are all healing our own scars and fighting our own battles We are kind almost all the time whenever we get the chance." And why I was saying that I do not know. Perhaps it was a reflection of my own needs.

It was late when we got back to the apartment. We sat down in the living room and shortly afterward Joe joined us. He had two joints and offered us one. Sleeping arrangements had not been made yet. Joe offered me a place on the floor with a sleeping bag. Jane had an extra mattress in her little room. It didn't take me long to make my choice. We said goodnight to Joe and closed the door.

Again, I became philosophical and said, "I hope you are not lost and are finding your own way. Remember as we go through a life lesson with another soul, we both grow. We are not given a good life or a bad life. We are given a life. It is up to us to make it good or bad. Only my opinion of my life is the most important one." We talked long into the night.

Next morning Jane made us coffee. While we sat together at the small kitchen table sipping our steamy strong brew, I wanted to express my feelings so we could create a platform in order to come closer to each other.

"I have not seen you before, but I feel I have known you for years. You are the kind of person I've always wanted to be associated with and maybe we are meant for each other. I believe in pre-destiny." I went on and on and finally I said, "You are the kind of person I've been looking for."

That started a long, involved discussion about continuing our relationship and after several more cups of coffee, it was time for me to leave. That was difficult. We hugged each other warmly with hopes of meeting again soon.

One month before my father died, I received a letter from him asking why I was not interested in marriage. There were several families offering their daughters for marriage and my father needed to give them an explanation.

"Please express your intentions," he wrote and, "when are you coming to India?"

I did not write to my father but wrote to my younger brother: "Please convey this message about marriage to our mother and father. I am too involved in my business to think of getting married at this time. As soon as my circumstances change, I will inform you and I will let you know when I can visit India."

In 1977, my father wrote and asked the same question.

I felt that the arranged marriage route in India was like shopping for clothes. I was a twenty-nine-year old Hindu Brahmin male wanting a girl who was willing to settle in the U.S. rather than India. My parents, however, were looking for a suitable Indian girl who would live with me in my hometown of Gwalior. Unlike other Indian men, I was not interested in that lifestyle. I probably was not a good catch for any Indian woman anyway, because she might think I ate meat, which I don't, find me highly independent and opinionated, which I am, therefore, clearly classifying me as an "outcast" in the Indian marriage market.

After meeting Jane, I filed for a divorce from Shelly, the woman I had married in Chicago. It was granted in six weeks with no problems. Now, I was free to re-marry and to create my own family. Jane was on my mind. I wanted to get to know her more to convince myself that we could live a long-term joyful life. Our first meeting already impressed me and the image of her was constantly on my mind. Since there was no Hindu *Pundit* (priest) to approve our astrological match which favors our existence through planetary systems, I invited Jane to visit me in Denver where I could check out her "aura" more closely.

There are 32 GUNA (qualities of a person) to be matched before marriage, called *Kundali* match. *Kundali* is a chart which contains all information about a person's "*grah*" (planets) and their positions in different houses affecting different areas of life. It is stated in our scriptures and *Vedas* (science of life) that persons with a larger number of matches results in a fruitful marriage. If "*gunas*" are not matching in the "*Kundali*," then it means there is lower chance of compatibility. Thus, there is a lesser chance of marriage survival.

Those who believe in Hinduism, trust that the Planets in the sky rule the world. When there is movement of Sun from one *Raasi* to another *Raasi* (an astrological sign) there are changes like calamities and accidents. The Hindus believe in the power of the Full Moon (strength) and New Moon (weakness). Many people don't perform marriages or other auspicious ceremonies on the New Moon.

I was happy Jane accepted my invitation and she flew to Denver as planned. My major concern was her lifestyle and eating habits. We came from two very different backgrounds and I wanted to make sure we understood each other.

After her visit, I went to the Hindu temple to find positive support. I needed to know if I was going in the right direction in marrying Jane, a non-devotee of Krishna. I received cloudy and confusing opinions by various members of the ISKCON (International Society for Krishna Consciousness) community.

But my inner soul was speaking in a positive direction and my personal opinion was more important. I needed to live my life my way. I knew I was looking for friendship, a family of my own, sexual intimacy, self-esteem, honor and creativity; I felt Jane was looking for the same thing. Even though I wasn't able to find the right answer, I felt confident that we could create another lifestyle that would work for both of us.

Within a week of her visit, I flew to San Francisco. We were walking on Telegraph Ave. in Berkeley quite near the ISKCON Temple when I turned to her most respectfully and asked her if we could marry. I felt we were destined for each other. Happily, she said, "Yes!"

Seven Circles ... Jane

MARRIAGE: A BONDING OF a man and a woman for better and for worse. In Hinduism I believe it has a stronger, more dedicated and more complex meaning.

I was not sure what I was getting myself into when I said "yes" to Pradeep's proposal of marriage. At the time, my life was unsettled, and I had to make some decisions.

I had worked since I was fourteen, paid for my college education, traveled to many countries and driven across the USA several times. Many of these trips, I traveled by myself. I moved to California and always found employment as a teacher, but now I was unemployed. Perhaps, it was time to have a partner, to have someone with whom to share my life. I questioned whether marriage was what I actually needed and how committed was I to this union? Pradeep was so enthusiastic and reassuring when "yes" popped out of my mouth, that I eventually embraced my decision and became quite excited about the prospects of becoming his wife. With that anticipation, however, there developed another sensation ... that of panic: "What do I really know about his culture, and what he personally thinks? I'm a free spirit. Will I still be free? Do I want to be free?"

I put these thoughts on hold while I planned the wedding. We agreed that the ceremony should represent both of us.

The pastor of my church gladly agreed to perform the Christian part of the ceremony and he willingly acknowledged the Hindu ceremony.

Pradeep's Hindu wedding traditions were a little more elaborate, colorful, and stringent. He planned the Hindu ceremony with his sister, Kusum who would be flying in from London with her two daughters.

Sewing and designing my wedding dress and his shirt were a way for me to express myself and I could share this part of me with Pradeep. I traveled around San Francisco looking for the right fabrics, and found a Folk Wear pattern, an Afghan Wedding Gown that would fit the occasion perfectly. We wanted an uplifting, lively wedding, representing this joyous event: music, good food, and laughter with family and friends

The date was set for March 10, 1979 at my home in Gardner, Massachusetts. My mother would take care of the food and a Finnish friend of the family volunteered to make the wedding cake; her infamous carrot cake. Most of my friends lived on Martha's Vineyard, a tiny island off the coast of Massachusetts, and when they heard about my engagement, they were excited to take part.

Leaving behind my old life, I flew to the East Coast.

Before going home to Gardner, I took the bus to Woods Hole on Cape Cod and boarded a ferry to Martha's Vineyard where my friend Eleanor greeted me. With great excitement and anticipation, we gathered our friends together and proceeded to delve into planning "Jane's exotic wedding."

A group of us had worked for Bill Smith's Clambakes out of Edgartown, and they were eager to help out. My friend Alan played the guitar and agreed to provide the music. Pradeep and I wanted something lively, jazzy He was instructed not to play the traditional "wedding march." He agreed. My friend, Malcolm volunteered to be the photographer. His most recent interest was photography and with his newly purchased camera was eager to take the wedding pictures.

Three weeks before the wedding, I called the Colonial Inn in Concord, Massachusetts, to make reservations for our wedding night. I expected the wedding suite would be arranged for us. The receptionist was pleasant, and the reservation was confirmed. Pradeep had informed me that he would have to leave for Denver the next day after the wedding because of some business he had to tend to, but we would have the evening together. That meant, I would have more time with my family and my friend Mary, from California, before I left for Denver and the planned honeymoon trip "around the world." Mary, whom I had lived with in Ben Lomond, California, joined me a couple of days before the ceremony to be close at hand. I needed a little support. I wasn't quite sure this was the right thing to do. Perhaps this decision had been made in haste. Should we have acted so fast? It was too late to think of that now. Everyone was coming very soon to see me get married.

The day of the wedding, before the guests arrived, Mary and I sat on my bed in my childhood bedroom. I was dressed in my white Afghani wedding dress and we sat in silence. I stared at the dainty flowered wallpaper of green, violet and white, remembering how my mother, many years ago, wanted to surprise me with a newly decorated room when I came home from Girl Scout Camp. She wallpapered the walls, bought a violet bedspread, placed ruffles around the bottom of the bed and bought a cute vanity table with a mirror. It was so "girly." I hated it. Now as I gazed at my room, I thought how lovely and feminine it was and that's exactly how I felt.

The house was filled with friends and family. My mother hustled about, finishing up the last-minute food preparations. Her silver-blue hair was flipped at the ends and she was dressed to perfection, even though she wore an apron wrapped around her green satin dress. She appeared satisfied with the way the house looked and if she had any doubts of her daughter's choice of husband, she made no sign of it. The guests were packed into the living room waiting eagerly for the ceremony to begin. The Pastor, dressed in his white robe, stood in front of the bay window in the living room waiting for the music to start. Alan should have been in the front ready to play the uplifting, jazzy song that he had rehearsed. From the back of the room, I could hear a faint strumming. He was strumming the melody of Mendelssohn's "Wedding March!" I stood there amongst my guests, bewildered and disappointed. I couldn't move, but with a big smile on his face, Pradeep took my hand, gave me a little tug and off we danced down the aisle (I think he was stoned but I wasn't sure). And wasn't I supposed to walk down the aisle with my stepfather? Oh, well. The pastor gave a short, lovely and endearing proclamation of love and marriage and Pradeep and I said, "I do."

The Hindu part of the ceremony followed. Pradeep's sister, Kusum, placed colorful garlands around our necks, and wrapped us together in a red, silver-embroidered sari. Everyone was clapping and cheering as we slowly walked the Seven Circles, each circle representing a different blessing from God. Kusum explained to the onlookers what each circle represented. Traditionally, the couple walked around a fire but, of course, we could not have a fire inside the house. Another Hindu wedding custom had the guests throwing *ghee* (clarified butter) into a fire and giving the bride and groom a blessing. A small fire was built on our front stone porch. We gathered around as people lined up to receive their spoonful of *ghee* to throw into the fire. My uncle Bud, on the other hand, who apparently did not listen to the instructions, did not know what to do with it and ate his spoonful of *ghee*.

The wedding was delightful, and my family and friends experienced a wedding tradition from a different culture, which they happily embraced. The only thing missing from this lovely day was the jazzy music.

When the day came to an end, Pradeep and I said our goodbyes to everyone, and we left for Concord as husband and wife. We checked into the hotel, trying not to be too giddy, opened the door to our honeymoon suite and were confronted with two twin beds in a small room. We were amused and a little disappointed that the honeymoon accommodations weren't a bit more romantic, but the mattress on the floor worked just fine.

Seven Circles ... Pradeep

MY SISTER KUSUM AND her two daughters would be flying in from London. Kusum accepted my marriage to Jane and promised not to say anything to the rest of the family until I explained the situation to our mother. I was hoping that, with my sister and her daughters present, the wedding would be joyful, and Jane's family would accept me. It was important that any doubts should be removed from anybody's mind because tomorrow we would become family.

My mother trained me with sacraments called "*sanskars*" and, in her absence Jane and I performed a '*Vivah Sanskars*' which marked the start of the most important stage of our lives. It is called "*Grihistha Ashram*" which involves setting up a new family life. Two individuals, considered to be compatible for a lifelong partnership, have a ceremony during which the household responsibilities and duties of each are explained. The precise details and rituals performed in our wedding ceremony were a variation pertaining to my home in Gwalior.

The main stages of our wedding were: First, the bride's parents, Ruth and Ralph welcome the bridegroom and his family at the house where the wedding is to take place. A red "*Kum-kum*" powder is applied to their foreheads. Members of each family are now introduced. In this case it was my older sister, Kusum, who took the place of my mother. The introduction of the two families marks the start of a relationship between the two partial families without both mothers together.

My mother was in India and would not have agreed to support this marriage. She was not ready to let the people in her community know that Jane and I accepted each other willingly, voluntarily and pleasantly. My mother was expected to give her daughter-in-law an auspicious necklace, *Mangla Sootra. Mangla Sootra* was the emblem of marital status of a Hindu woman. This exchange did not happen. I could not introduce my mother, but other family members were introduced, hoping that in time my mother might give up the traditional part of Hinduism and develop a new understanding of the modern world.

The best way to start a married life is to establish an honest relationship. I had said to Jane, "We are important, and we are deserving. You are intelligent, loving, beautiful, creative, inspiring and true and able to realize this for yourself. I have realized that I am brave, strong, worthy and compassionate. So, let us materialize the wedding ceremony on March 10, 1979." It was time to speak with the spiritual light, over and above all words, "Jane, speak to yourself with your own light and speak to me with the light that you are and never forget that with every choice we each make we create our own lives."

I believe that good things are going to happen and everything I need will come to me at the perfect time. I never told Jane "I love you" because I understood that love is not some- thing we do, love is something that we are. It can be felt without telling each other. My older brother once told me, "Wise men don't love the most beautiful girl in the world, they love the girl who can make their world the most beautiful."

On March 10th, I told myself, today is my day to let go of things that no longer serve me. Marrying Jane is the most courageous decision I have ever made. I need to let go of what has been hurting my heart and soul. I was using all "three eyes" (the third eye is the spiritual eye) and everything was alive during the seven circles.

The guests were curious to know more about the Hindu wedding ceremony, what it entailed and signified. The joy and exuberance were evident at our wedding and were unparalleled to other various ceremonies and sacred rituals. I explained that the most significant ritual was that of the "Seven Circles" performed around an open fire.

In Hindu religion, it is believed that the fire or heat is the maintainer of life. The bride and groom are required to take this ritual together around the holy fire which represents a part of God in each of them.

Kusum was prepared to perform the ritual under her guidance as a priest. We weren't able to have a fire inside the house, but we managed to make the circles around each other.

First Circle: *The couple pray to God that He will extend blessings upon them; blessings of healthy food and respectful life. Both promise that their love shall become more intense with each passing day and to help each other in every possible* *manner. We promised to fulfill responsibilities to our family with utmost care and dedication. We will take care of our honor and remain bound to our love forever.*

Second Circle: *We plead to God for imparting us with mental stability, physical health and spiritual strength. That this pure relationship as man and wife will be forever.*

Third Circle: *As a couple, we both invoke God to provide us with uttermost wealth, wisdom, and prosperity.*

Fourth Circle: *We, as a couple, pray to God for bestowing happiness and rapport on us. It signifies the importance of family, parents and elders. Bringing out a commitment between two souls that they will remain pledged to take care of elders, family members, and parents for the rest of their lives.*

Fifth Circle: *We, as a couple, pray to the Almighty to bless with his kindness all living things of this universe. We also pray for happiness and well-being of each other's relatives and friends.*

Sixth Circle: *We, as a couple, implore for a long, joyous life and togetherness.*

Seventh Circle: *The couple begs God for a life-long lasting bond enriched with good understanding, loyalty, and companionship. We pledge to bear the relationship with love and honesty. The couple invokes and prays for social welfare as well as universal peace.*

So, on this day, Jane and I prayed for a joyful life. With the Seven Circles completed, our existence was now entirely devoted to each other. I was completely in her heart and she in mine.

Chicken Casserole ... Jane

PRADEEP FOUND US AN apartment on the east side of Denver. The apartment building stood four stories high: simple with well-kept grounds and lobby. As we entered the elevator to go to the 4th floor I noticed no other people. When the elevator door opened, we were greeted with a long empty corridor: too quiet. We stopped in front of #402, opened the door and gazed upon three sparsely furnished rooms: a living room, kitchen and a bedroom with the bathroom located off the bedroom. All were small and painted white. The couch was beige as well as the carpet.

Living in an apartment building had never appealed to me before and certainly not now, especially up on the 4th floor. I had always gravitated to the first floor where I'd have access to the ground: gardens, patios; outside space. This apartment felt claustrophobic. Because we were leaving for Europe in a month, I packed only what I needed for the trip. How was I going to cope living in this empty box without my belongings? I kept reminding myself that we were there for a short time until business issues were settled. I was usually flexible when it came to living situations; after all, I had just left a closet in San Francisco. As long as Pradeep and I were together, setting up housekeeping, and remaining enchanted with each other, I told myself, things would be fine.

The first few days, when Pradeep came home from the agency, we would prepare dinner together and talk. He loved to cook. He showed me how to create Indian vegetarian dishes using curry, cumin and turmeric. The apartment filled with tantalizing smells. My favorite morning ritual was the making of chai, a spicy hot tea.

First, Pradeep would boil up a cup of water in which he added one heaping tablespoon of fresh ginger, four or five peppercorns, some cardamom seeds and a tablespoon of tea. Next, he added a cup of milk and some sugar, letting it boil up again, then he let it simmer for a few minutes. He stirred the mixture constantly, so it wouldn't boil over. He'd then pour the tea through a strainer into our cups and we would sip the aromatic, delicious drink.

I had this astonishing realization that my Scandinavian heritage and his Hindu culture had something in common: *cardamon*. It is a spice grown in India and highly used in Indian cooking. It is also used in Sweden for baking *kardemummabullar* (sweet bun) and in Finnish *pulla* (sweet bread).

We spent the first few days comfortable, happy. Then he began coming home later in the evenings. He seemed stressed and detached. We had no telephone so he couldn't contact me when he was running late. He explained that there were some problems with the agency but never explained what the problems were.

He became possessive of me: not wanting me to leave the building without him or walk into town alone. The days became boring and lonely.

At this time I noticed I was tired and feeling nauseous in the morning. I was pregnant. A friend of mine lived in Denver so I called her to ask if she could recommend a doctor. She too was pregnant and arranged an appointment for us to go to the clinic together. We also agreed we would meet for dinner some evening soon.

In the basement of the apartment building was a swimming pool. In order to keep my sanity and to keep my body in shape, I swam every day. I swam alone with the whisper of my strokes and the rhythm of my breathing. I'd float on my back staring at the ceiling far above me in a trance, relaxed, as if I were floating in a bubble.

How could a liberated, independent woman like me, who had traveled around Europe and Central America alone, now find herself in a situation where she couldn't even take a walk around the neighborhood? I had assumed Pradeep was accustomed to the American ways and I had expected to make up my own mind about certain matters. I should have familiarized myself more thoroughly with Indian marriage customs. I was concerned.

One day I called my Denver friend and she invited me for dinner. She cooked up a delicious chicken casserole. Having the evening out lifted my spirits. Talking and laughing soothed my anxiety.

I figured I'd be home before Pradeep because he had been coming home so late, but when I arrived, he was already there. I was happy and wanted to tell him about my evening, but my excitement came to a halt when I told him I had eaten chicken. He became enraged; yelling, pacing back and forth, flailing his arms, saying I was contaminated, and he couldn't kiss me or make love to me for three days.

Now, where was that coming from? I didn't realize I was not allowed to eat meat while I was married to him! I knew he was a vegetarian, but I didn't know how strict, and how it was connected to Hinduism. I had chosen to be a vegetarian for a year or two in the past, just to have the experience of no meat in my diet. There were no special health concerns or religious rules. I respected his choice of diet and would not cook meat in our kitchen if it were to interfere with his beliefs, but, on the other hand, I wanted to eat my mother's meatballs if I chose to do so. I think we had a few more things to discuss about traditions and customs of our two cultures. I can't remember if that was the night that I lost it, but one night I started screaming and throwing pots and pans at him. I locked myself in the bathroom and cried.

Obviously, communication lacked between us. His smoking hash or stress at work factored into my questioning this relationship. I realized I had just married a man, for better and for worse, who, I felt, demonstrated irrational behavior.

The baby growing inside me rebelled. After our confrontation regarding the "chicken casserole," I began spotting. With tension growing between us, I felt it would be helpful if I visited my friend Mary in Ben Lomond. Mary was a nurse and if I encountered any further complications, she would be close by. Pradeep and I would have time to gather our thoughts and calm down before our honeymoon.

I flew to San Francisco, picked up my car from my brother's in Fremont and drove south to Santa Cruz. The miscarriage came quickly. I drove frantically to the hospital where the ER staff admitted me. At first, they wanted me to fill out a stack of papers but when they noticed the state I was in, they proceeded to rush me onto a gurney to be wheeled off for a D&C. The child was not meant to be. I cried and grieved with mixed emotions.

Of course, Pradeep had no knowledge of what happened. Only when I felt ready did I finally call him from the hospital.

His receptionist answered the phone. She sounded nervous, not her usual friendly self, and told me Pradeep was not there. I explained to her where I was and gave her the phone number. I expected to chat a little as we had done many times before but this time she abruptly hung up. Not at all like her. At some point, Pradeep called, and I told him about the miscarriage. Of course, he felt terrible and hoped I was doing well.

But he too had bad news.

Greg had asked him to go to the mountains outside of Denver, a trip they often made on weekends. When they returned to the city, they found out that someone had set fire to the agency. And the day before, while I had been talking with the receptionist on the phone, someone was robbing the place and had a gun to her head! I had so many questions and my emotions, needless to say, were in an overwhelmed and chaotic state. But I couldn't help thinking that the series of incidences at the agency, happening right before our honey- moon, weren't quite right, perhaps, even suspicious.

After leaving Dominican Hospital I spent several more days recuperating at Mary's home. On the drive back to my brother's in Fremont, I tried to dismiss the barrage of misfortunes of the past few weeks and envisioned my future in a positive way. Before Pradeep could join me in Fremont, he had to settle matters with the fire department, police, detectives, and insurance agents.

Chicken Casserole … Pradeep

THE APARTMENT I RENTED was small and simple, but most important to me was having a decent kitchen. Here we cooked tasty spicy Indian food which Jane and I both enjoyed. In the morning, I would make chai, hot, steaming and fragrant.

On weekends we would walk around Capitol Hill or drive to the mountains.

However, Jane was getting bored sitting in the apartment all day while I worked during the week and she decided to visit her friend Mary in Santa Cruz. The day before she left, she met with a high school friend for dinner. I was unaware of her having a dinner engagement, and it concerned me that she was not home. With her being pregnant, I worried. I pre- pared a few Indian dishes for dinner and when Jane returned, she explained she had already eaten dinner with her friend who had made a chicken casserole. It was good to know she was safe, but it upset me to know she had eaten meat. We proceeded to have a confrontation about the differences in our eating habits. That led her to be uncomfortable with her thoughts, in other words, she too was clearly upset.

In 1973 I flew back to India where I met with my uncle, Vidya. He asked if I had any problems in America.

"Yes," I said. "Being a vegetarian. People ask me why I'm a vegetarian and I don't know why. Throughout the generations, our family have always been vegetarian."

My wise uncle replied:

"Nature has created two types of creatures on the Earth. Nature has created a territory: on one side, creatures drink water by sucking and nails are flat; on the other side of the territory, creatures drink water by licking and nails are sharp like claws. All creatures who suck water are vegetarians, elephants, horses and man, etc. All creatures who lick water eat meat, cats, dogs and tigers, etc. and they all remain in their territory."

For me, it was clear that all humans should be vegetarian and that it was important to respect the Law of Nature to avoid unnecessary complications. It was difficult to think of sharing my kitchen with a "meat-eater." Perhaps we would need to have two different kitchens. I could sense that Jane would not agree to a strict vegetarian diet for herself. Then I thought that I cannot take somebody's food away until I offer to make vegetarian food for them.

The next morning, I made chai. Jane stood by and watched as she had done many times before. We were calm.

We sipped our tea in silence. Then I left for the office. I returned at noon to prepare a nice lunch, saying humorously, "I'll make us a lunch without chicken!" She did not find that funny, thought of it as sarcasm. She flew off the handle causing distress for herself and me. She left for Santa Cruz angry.

World Ways Travel Company... Pradeep

WHILE JANE WAS PREPARING for the wedding, I was running around, organizing the transport of the buses for the overland journey from Munich to Gwalior that I had purchased and settling charter flights. We would be gone for two and a half months and I wanted everything to run smoothly while I was away. I periodically checked in with the agency to see if anyone needed help or had questions. All seemed to be fine.

I also had on my mind the political disturbances in India resulting in my father's murder. I needed to arrange family protection and to keep in contact with high officials including Mrs. Indira Gandhi, who had considered my father a highly valuable person in her administration.

Before Jane and I planned to get married, Scout decided to take over his family's Italian shoe store. That left me with an empty position. Scout suggested Greg, to do the accounting, and assist the agency's sales team. He would collect money from the customers and make deposits into the University National Bank of Denver.

I prided myself in running a financially sound professional business with ethical and moral responsibility with a competent staff:

Greg: Indian-born, legal, permanent resident of the USA. Greg and I met at a Seven-Eleven where he worked, and he mentioned he was looking for a better job. We developed a friendship and I hired him as an outside salesperson. He turned out to be beneficial because he had several community contacts. Within six months, he proved to be an efficient and trustworthy salesperson and I promoted him to a Travel Counselor (a person who gives information and quotes ticket prices). Before Scout left, he recommended Greg to supervise other outside sales and do liaison work. That meant Greg would be able to deposit checks and pick up blank airline tickets that were secured in the bank. He worked with Janet who was sales manger.

Janet: American. Experienced travel agent with excellent references. I hired her to be an airline ticket and reservation manager, authorized to do bank transactions, refund customers, pay office bills, and handle employees and public relations. Hard working, responsible.

Max: Australian National, legal permanent resident of USA. He had worked for Quantas Airlines and I needed extra help during the summer season when it became very busy, I hired him to help Janet with managerial tasks. In 1979, I authorized him to operate a separate account with a sufficient amount of money to offer claims and refunds.

Jacoline: Arabian/American, trained as a Travel Counselor ... a charming young lady with good communication skills.

Lee: Korean/American, hired as an Outside Salesman to reach out to the Asian community.

Tony: African American, former police officer, hired to supervise illegal or unauthorized activity within the agency; a security guard, overseeing the safety of the employees and the contents of the office.

Faizal: Pakistan National permanent resident of USA lived in Chicago but would come during the busy season to help with accounting and bookkeeping.

Susan: American, Travel Counselor.

Tanya: Mexican American, a Travel Counselor and consultant.

Martha: American, experienced bookkeeper.

However, life throws some punches.

The robbery took place around 3:30 pm on Saturday. Jacoline was alone at the office. Normally, Tony would have been there, but he was in New York.

She was sitting at the desk nearest the front door when a black man came in and took a gun out of his pocket. He pointed the gun at her head and wanted to know where Pradeep was. At that moment, the telephone rang, and he motioned her to answer it. It was Jane calling from the Dominican Hospital in Santa Cruz to tell me about her miscarriage. Jacoline was terrified. She tried her best to communicate with Jane, but she could barely speak and hung up. Jacoline told the man that I was on my lunch break and would be back shortly. He told her to take him downstairs but changed his mind and ran out the door.

When I returned to the office and saw her in a state of panic. I immediately called the police. They came and asked questions but had no luck finding the culprit.

That evening, Greg came to my apartment and suggested we drive to Dillon to relax from the unsettling event of the day. We often took off for the mountains on weekends. Much later that night, an arsonist set fire to the agency.

By the time we reached World Ways Travel, Sunday morning, the fire had been extinguished. Glass from the front of the building indicated that some type of explosion occurred, blowing the glass well out into the middle of the street.

The building was a one-story structure on the east side of an alley. Other buildings were attached in a row, but the fire did not extend to those structures, only smoke. The front door was locked, and there was no sign of a break-in which concerned me because only four people had keys: Greg, Max, Tony and myself. In the manager's office was a metal safe which was wide open and on the floor were strewn numerous scorched papers, tickets and travel records. In the corner of this room a two-gallon gasoline can was lying on its side, the neck and spout melted by the heat of the blaze. The investigators were unable to connect anyone to the fire.

The next day I talked with the fire department and with one of the investigators to see if they had any more information. They were still searching the area and had no new clues. While the investigation continued, I arranged enough money for Max to make refunds to people whom we could not serve and to relocate our travel agency to another building. Fortunately, I was able to salvage some important documents, but, at the same time, others equally pertinent were lost. So, before Jane and I left on our honeymoon, I took some time to re-establish the books.

The police told me I was free to go on my trip. The business, in its new location, seemed stable and my presence was not needed at this time. I flew to San Francisco to join Jane at her brother's where we would prepare for our "around the world honeymoon trip."

The Suitcase ... Jane

WHEN PRADEEP ARRIVED AT my brother's, he walked in with a duffel bag and an old battered brown leather suitcase. We hugged, holding each other in a long embrace, letting our differences lay behind us. I led him into the bedroom where we would be staying and as I helped him unpack, I asked about the brown suitcase which I had not seen before.

"What's in the suitcase?"

"Money," he said nonchalantly.

"Money? How much?" I asked, curiously.

"$30,000," he said.

I really thought he was joking but when he opened the suitcase, there it was, $30,000 in crisp dollar bills tied up in neat little bundles just like you would see in a gangster movie after a bank robbery.

"How did you get all that money and what are you planning to do with it?" I gasped in disbelief.

"It's my savings and we're going to bury it," he said.

"And where?" I asked with as much attitude as I could

muster.

He hesitated, "In your brother's back yard."

He explained that in India people bury their money because the banks are so corrupt. I had read about this, but to bury money in the USA, that was unheard of. Reluctantly, I went along with his decision.

My brother and sister-in-law were at work and their children were in school. It was early afternoon which meant we had a couple of hours before anyone returned home. First, we wrapped the money in tinfoil, lots of tinfoil, and then wrapped it in a paper bag. We found a shovel in the garage, decided upon a spot in the garden and dug a hole. We placed the money in the hole, covered the bundle with dirt, packed it down with our feet camouflaging it with leaves and loose soil. Exhausting, but the deed was done.

The money stayed in the garden for two days. On the third day, Pradeep informed me that he didn't feel comfortable about his decision and said the money had to be moved elsewhere. I didn't understand why he changed his mind, but I went along with his new plan. We dug it all up and transferred the bundles of hundreds of dollars into my backpack. We then gathered our luggage and took a taxi to BART (Bay Area Rapid Transit, rail service). He contrived another plan: head for San Francisco, bury the money in Golden Gate Park and catch a plane to London which would be the beginning of our two-and-a-half-month honeymoon.

Carrying thirty thousand dollars around on my back rattled my nerves. Paranoia set in as I sat on BART that day. What was I thinking? I wanted wooing. I wanted romance. I had just gotten married and so far, life with my new husband seemed not just questionable but a bit uncertain.

When we reached San Francisco, we checked into the Ritz Carlton Hotel and immediately hopped on a local bus headed for Golden Gate Park. This time Pradeep carried the money. We got off at the end of the line and headed toward the water. On the edge of a cliff facing the Pacific Ocean was a granite bench. I sat down. He walked alone toward the park with the money on his back. I refused to accompany him on his mission.

As I sat beneath the clear blue sky, I looked out onto the Pacific Ocean where the water sparkled in the sunlight. To my right I could see in the distance the Cliff House resting on the cliff like a steadfast castle, a must-see if visiting San Francisco. To my left, 100 feet away was Golden Gate Park where Pradeep recently entered. The air was clear and fresh. *Everything will be just fine*, I reassured myself. I wanted to believe I had made the right choice; that I had married a good man. I remembered reading somewhere, "He is good at being good and good at being bad." I began to believe that that was an accurate characterization of my beloved husband. I dismissed the fact that he was on his way to bury $30,000 cash in a park and convinced myself that it was an OK thing to do. I stared out at the beautiful view in front of me and settled into a state of complacency and denial.

In less than an hour, I saw his figure approaching. When he reached the bench, he sat down beside me, the backpack empty.

"Are you ready to go now?" he asked. I nodded.

We stood up, he took my hand and we headed for the bus stop.

I called my brother to let him know we would be going to London in a few days. Apparently, the police had been to his house and wanted to know the whereabouts of a Mr.

Parashar. Paul did not know where we were and told me Pradeep needed to call the police and answer their questions.

I had left my VW Bug with my brother and whenever he drove it, he noticed a police car would follow him. I have to mention that my car was a traveling piece of art-work. It was painted bright blue with a metallic green hood and on the hood was painted a brilliant yellow sunburst, impossible to miss.

Paul and his wife Sue lived in a neat middle-class community, and having this car sitting in front of their house caused anxiety for my brother and his family. He was doing me a great favor by looking after my "hippie mobile" while I was traveling. The neighbors were curious why the car was there and why the police were lurking around. Perhaps the police thought Paul would lead them to Pradeep ... who knows?

Pradeep said he made a phone call to the police and reassured me that everything was alright. After that, we packed our bags and immediately left for the airport.

I needed to make a choice. Marriage with this man had become more complicated than I could ever have imagined, but more than that, had caused a perplexing dilemma: do I go with him or do I walk away? For better or for worse is what I had agreed upon. Foolish or not, I decided to go with him to see what fate had in store. I grabbed his hand and we ran for a taxi.

The Suitcase ... Pradeep

JET SET TRAVEL AGENCY signed up to manage outside sales while I was away. I planned on expanding the business in Europe, and the Greyhound Buses were about to be shipped to Frankfurt for the opening of a new tourist bus service called "Bus Stop Tours" from Frankfurt to Goa via Srinagar, New Delhi and Agra, the other bus coming from Munich to Gwalior via New Delhi and Agra

Jane was not familiar with my business activities but did express interest in supporting the growth of the tourist bus service. She remained in Fremont with her brother preparing for our honeymoon.

Things were moving at a fast rate. Soon we were to embark on an around-the-world adventure/business trip. I was concerned with Jane's health after her miscarriage and also thinking as newlyweds that we should have spent more time together earlier. But, because she was a mature, well-educated woman, I figured she would understand my business and frequent absences.

I missed her greatly and wanted to join her in Fremont as soon as possible but needed to organize the trip first. I planned a combination business/honeymoon trip because

I wanted to show her how I had traveled from India to Europe, seeing different countries and to stop in Frankfurt to make arrangements for establishing our new business.

I looked at my budget for the trip and had enough credit but needed cash in hand. I went to the University National Bank in Denver and withdrew $50,000, my savings from the previous year. Credit cards could pay for food and hotels.

I packed my suitcases, one with clothes and one filled with

$30,000 cash. The remaining money was in cash or Traveler's Checks and when I was ready, made my way to Fremont to join Jane.

Staying with her brother's family for a couple of days would be fine but I thought we'd have more privacy and independence if we stayed at a nice hotel in the city before we left on our trip. I needed to put the money somewhere safe before we went to San Francisco. So, we buried it in her brother's back yard in the corner of the garden. During our stay in the city, the "chicken casserole" came up again. It planted a seed of distrust with Jane and I felt I needed to put the money somewhere else.

My thoughts were: "If she does it my way, all would be fine, but if not, it will be difficult." The honeymoon trip was an important time to get to know each other. I wanted her to respect my vegetarianism. I wanted her to know God as I knew God, a vegetarian.

We returned to Fremont and dug up the money. After packing it in Jane's backpack, we took BART back to San Francisco and I buried the money in some remote part of Golden Gate Park. Jane did not want to help me and waited on a bench overlooking the Pacific Ocean. The money was my savings. I now felt it was safe and on my return from our trip, I would invest it toward my business.

With the money secure, we were ready to fly to London ahead of schedule. I asked Jane if she was ready to go now. She said "Yes."

It was May 15, 1979.

"Bus Stop Tours" ... Jane

WE WERE TIRED AND hungry when we finally arrived in London, but Pradeep insisted we walk to a nearby park where he could buy some hash. I couldn't believe it! Then after the drug transaction, we stopped at a small restaurant and later booked into a hotel. Again things were not comfortable between us. We were irritable and cranky. In a moment of rage, he accused me of not being much of a woman because I couldn't carry his child (referring to my miscarriage) and stormed out the room. Devastated, I wept and, at that point, didn't care if he came back or not. Obviously, our communication skills were lacking. Perhaps, the next day would be better. We met up with his sister, Kusum and her daughters, went sightseeing in London and ate delicious Indian food in Russell Square.

Pradeep and I dismissed the battle of the night before and toured London happily as a newly married couple. Finally, a sense of normalcy set in.

A few days later, we flew to Frankfurt, Germany. Somehow, Pradeep managed to rent an apartment where we stayed for a week. It was centrally located and within walking distance to shopping, beer halls and restaurants.

One day while strolling around, we noticed a VW bus for sale and decided to buy it in order to travel through Europe by car. The bus had a little stove, portable toilet and a folding bed and lots of room for our stuff, which meant we could travel wherever and whenever we wanted. We bought cooking supplies, food, maps and began planning our trip through Germany, Switzerland, Italy and Yugoslavia.

When the van was packed, we headed for Munich.

One day, we parked the bus on a street in front of the University of Munich and prepared our afternoon lunch. Of course, we cooked Indian food and the delightful aromas filled the air. Many people gathered around the van watching us cook and asking questions about how and what we were making. We were enjoying ourselves, but the police did not appreciate our presence in the busy parking area in front of the school and asked us to leave.

We then drove through Switzerland on windy, steep, mountainous, often terrifying roads and continued on to Italy where our drive was much more relaxing. We slept in olive groves and vineyards, found cozy cafes in which to sip wine or drink espresso coffee. The beauty of the hillsides and the quaint villas tucked into the rolling landscape were captivating. I was entranced and could have stayed much longer but we wanted to continue driving down the coast of Yugoslavia where we visited the city of Split. We then headed inland and north to Zagreb. In Zagreb, we stumbled upon a market where food, antiques, and handcrafted items were sold. I bought a hand-embroidered tablecloth, white with red embroidery, and a navy blue pleated short jacket with gold embroidery on the collar. Then we turned back north, toward Germany, where we prepared ourselves for the flight to India. This was a wonderful romantic segment of our honeymoon.

Back in Frankfurt, Pradeep met an Indian couple who were interested in Pradeep's idea of a business named "Bus Stop Tours." The two men discussed forming a partnership and a "deal" was made. We left our VW bus with the couple, with plans to return in a few months to work out details of the business. I looked forward to this new adventure and the opportunity of working in Frankfurt. My dream of a new career and travel just might come true.

I felt optimistic about our future.

"Bus Stop Tours" ... Pradeep

WE CHECKED INTO THE Grand Hotel in Kensington, an historical hotel convenient for walking and seeing the sights of London. Jane and I had a miscommunication when we first arrived but after visiting my sister, Kusum, and her two daughters, we worked it out. Kusum was our tour guide, showing us the famous sights, leading us to museums and delightful restaurants.

London to Frankfurt was a short flight. Once in the city, we settled in a middle range hotel in Frankfurt center. We walked along the "*strasses*" and happily got on and off the *Strassenbahn* (trolley). One day shortly after our arrival we ended up walking along a street where many cars had "FOR SALE" signs stuck on them. We discussed the choices of traveling, having a set itinerary or the freedom to see Europe in our own style.

Having our own transportation sounded like a perfect plan. Parked on the street was an affordable 1971 VW, a blue and white van equipped with everything we needed to travel comfortably throughout Europe: kitchenette, foldable bed which converted into a sofa and a portable toilet. We bought it on the spot. Of course, papers had to be passed according to German motor vehicle registration laws, and a license plate had to be transferred, but by the next day all was completed. Both of us were looking forward to cooking our own food and especially to brewing chai for those early morning drives. Our first stop would be somewhere in Italy.

After a long scenic route, we reached Milan. We stayed there for a few days and drove through Venice and on into Switzerland.

We took a side trip to Basel to visit a teacher whom I'd known from Gwalior when I was a child. Lodi was an active member of the Indo-American Friendship and Cultural Society, a group promoting exchanges between the different cultures of the East and West. I knew her address but had no idea what part of the city she lived in. I randomly took an exit off the main highway, and to my surprise her street was off to the left. What a coincidence! We found a small house with her name and number on the door. We walked up to the house and knocked. She answered and needless to say, was very surprised to see me standing there. Warmly, she greeted us and offered us tea. She seemed very pleased to see me and to meet my American wife. After a pleasant visit of stories of friends and family, Jane and I continued our journey to Zürich and Geneva.

We camped and cooked in the mountains surrounded by majestic vistas. It was a memorable experience, especially driving along the steep, narrow mountain roads near Interlaken, a skier's paradise. We still had time to travel to Yugoslavia. But first we stopped in Trieste, Florence, and Napoli. We sampled the robust Italian foods, drank their delicate wines, and found places in olive groves and vineyards to park our van for the night. One moonless night, in one of these olive groves, the van got stuck in the mud. Jane and I pushed and pulled but were unsuccessful in getting it out. Meanwhile, the dogs in the neighborhood joined us and created a lot of noise, barking and howling, making us quite nervous. Because the dogs made such a racket, it woke up the locals and several men came out of their homes to investigate what was happening. They saw our dilemma and helped us get the van out of the mud, saying nothing about the fact that we were sleeping in their olive grove.

Our routine when we drove into a new city was to park the van and walk around familiarizing ourselves with our new surroundings. When we reached Split, Yugoslavia, we parked the van in a quiet neighborhood outside the city limits Once we walked out of this area, however, it felt uncomfortable. The people on the streets were loud and rowdy. Disappointed and a little nervous, we retreated to our van. Here, we cooked our dinner, drank a bottle of wine and spent a relaxed evening in the safety of our neighborhood. Next day after breakfast we started our journey back to Germany.

When we arrived in Frankfurt, we had to think about selling the van. During our first visit we befriended an Indian man originally from Goa. We contacted him and were invited to dinner during which our host mentioned that he wanted to change his business as a merchant and focus on another occupation. I explained to him my plans for a tour business, providing tours from Frankfurt to Goa. I mentioned that I had already planned for two Greyhound buses to arrive in Germany as soon as the project was finalized. After further discussion, he became enthusiastic about investing in my business. He already had an office set up in Frankfurt and his family, who lived in Goa, could manage that end of the business. It was a major advantage for me too. Jane and I stayed in Frankfurt a few more days to firm up details and explore any difficulties that might arise. We agreed that the office should be moved to a more populated area in Frankfurt Main which would give us more exposure. We agreed on conditions, made legal agreements and a business deal was put into place. I gave him the van and some advance money for rent and office supplies. I felt comfortable with the business arrangement and was looking forward to returning after the honeymoon to this new business venture. Jane didn't understand everything that was going on but, all along, I had envisioned her as my "right hand man," and imagined her enjoying her new role as my assistant.

One of the best decisions we made was to travel through Europe in a VW van. We embraced diversity in languages, people, music, and food. We visited famous historical monuments, awed at temples and ornate churches, and walked in the mountains and along beaches. With fond memories, and a closer appreciation of each other, Jane and I flew to New Delhi to continue our honeymoon trip.

Mother Wouldn't Approve ... Jane

AT THE NEW DELHI train station I witnessed a scene of poverty: beggars sitting on the sides of the road, trash covering the tracks, crowds of people pushing, shoving, dust, and flies everywhere. Cars, rickshaws, and bicycles crowded the busy streets. No order to their movements. Chaos. Madness. I wanted to clean up all the little children, heal the old deformed women, and kick the police officer who took a stick to an old man lying in the gutter covered with flies. Sometimes I felt like vomiting. I was shocked and appalled.

Walking through the market section of the city, I experienced another way of Indian life: women with baskets filled with fresh fruits and vegetables balanced on their heads, carts loaded with bricks led by donkeys, vendors crowded next to each other, some making chai, others pressing sugarcane to make juice. The women and girls showed determination as they moved gracefully through the crowds to the market. Dressed in their bright colored saris, the women shopped, smiling, laughing, chatting. Booths filled with fabric serviced by men, offering women the finest of silks and cottons.

In fact most booths or shops were run by males.

The beauty and elegance of the Indian women impressed me. How could they move so freely with so much fabric wrapped around them?

We left New Delhi and headed north to Kashmir, our next destination. To my dismay, we boarded a local bus. That meant uncomfortable seats, crowded with people, perhaps animals, and no toilets! I was the only Westerner on board and felt clearly out of my comfort zone. My anxiety lessened when I learned that the bus driver stopped every few hours to let passengers out to relieve themselves. He would stop the bus on the side of the road, we'd all file out, find a spot and pee, the women to the right and the men to the left. No modesty here. Pradeep warned me ahead of time, so I wore a skirt and no underwear.

We arrived in Srinagar, the most northern state of Kashmir, on a beautiful sunny afternoon. Srinagar was located in a valley, looking upon the Pir Panjal Himalayan ranges, and rested on the sparkling waters of Dal Lake. Pradeep led me through the crowded streets to the houseboat we would be staying on for the week. From our houseboat there was a view of the mountains surrounding the lake. Scattered beneath the mountain range and along the water's edge were numerous temples, gardens, and mosques. A spectacular sight!

Once we settled in, Pradeep suggested having some clothes made for me in the local fashion. He took me to a tailor and within three days, I was presented with two *kurtas* (long shirts) and one pair of *pajama* pants. The fabric was beautiful and the garments well made. I thought I would blend in a little better with the locals if I dressed the way they did. Who was I kidding?

One extremely hot day, while we were being rowed around the lake in a *Shikara*, a long wooden narrow boat, I had the urge to jump in the water and that is what I did. The rower was aghast, and I think Pradeep was too. I should have known not to do this because the water wasn't exactly clean. People defecated and urinated in the water and washed their dishes and clothes in it. Though, in some parts, the lake was regarded as Holy Water. I never saw anyone else go for a "swim" nor did I ever go in again.

We spent a glorious week of exploring and relaxing and then headed south.

When we arrived in New Delhi, we were met by Pradeep's brother Rakesh. He was an active member of the Congress Party and managed to arrange for us to meet with Indira Gandhi. At this time Mrs. Gandhi was not Prime Minister. In 1977 she had been forced to resign and the opposing party, the Janata Party, had taken over. When Pradeep and I visited in 1979, she was rebuilding her power base and winning back the support of the Indian people.

A well-polished black sedan drove us to her bungalow on Race Course Road where many high officials resided. On our arrival, a security guard escorted us to a spacious room where several ornate wood carved chairs were placed against the walls. We waited a few minutes before he beckoned us to join her in her study, a small comfortable room with paintings on the walls, bookcases, a couch, and coffee table. She sat behind a big wooden well-polished desk and we were led to two chairs facing her. A huge French window brought in natural sunlight and she could look out to see who came and went. Security guards stood nearby. Mrs. Gandhi was soft-spoken and relaxed, well-poised, not too personal, but pleasant. She discussed her views on the current affairs and answered Pradeep's questions on the government's involvement in the world. She spoke in English, but I still didn't follow everything that she and Pradeep talked about. It certainly was the highlight of my trip. What an honor.

After leaving Mrs. Gandhi, our plan was to take a train to Gwalior where Pradeep grew up and where his mother and some of his siblings still lived, but first, we needed to exchange our money for rupees. Pradeep didn't want to go to the bank. He thought he would get a better exchange dealing on the "black market." We walked down a crowded alley, found a dealer and proceeded to get ripped off. The clever dealer folded the money in half as he counted the bills, making it look like he was counting the amount we asked for but actually, we received only half. Pradeep was furious with himself. He thought he was the clever one!

We proceeded to board the "first class" coach. When the conductor came along to collect our tickets, he told us we had the wrong tickets, yelled at us, and told us to board the "third class" coach. In other words, he kicked us off the train.

I was shocked when I saw the conditions of the "third class car." I labeled it "the cattle car." How could I ever travel like this? The people were crowded together, trunks and bags piled precariously on top of each other. Some passengers were sitting on top of their baggage. The car was narrow with no space to walk without stepping on someone or something. It was claustrophobic and I needed to be near fresh air or I might have a panic attack. We pushed and shoved our way past everyone to a sliding door where it was opened a crack. Breathing fresh air helped. And that is where we sat for the next five hours; cramped in like crayons in a box. I was not happy. One other thing upset me: getting to the toilet. It turned out to be a hole in the floor at the end of the corridor with no door or curtain. In order to get there, I had to climb over the other passengers and their trunks then push my way through the mass of men, women and children who were standing near the hole. I was the only white girl around and that day I had worn pants instead of a skirt, because I believed I would be traveling first class where there would be private toilets.

My fellow travelers were intensely curious about me, "the white foreigner" in their car. When I needed to use the toilet, all eyes followed me down the aisle and as I peed. I did the best I could to cover myself with my shirt and my shawl. It was intensely awkward and embarrassing. A trip from hell!

Pradeep attempted to make humor of my situation and eventually I, too, was able to laugh. The women and I nodded and smiled at each other. Pradeep translated, so we could have some communication. I truly felt warmth and compassion for my fellow travelers. They sat there calmly, no fussing, no whining, not even the children. I was humbled.

I relaxed once we reached Gwalior and settled into Hotel Tansen, a relatively new, clean, 3-star hotel. Pradeep's hometown appeared less busy and crowded compared to New Delhi, and as long as I was accompanied by a man, I was treated with respect and not hassled. We met with Rakesh who introduced me to his family and to his younger brother, Sunil. But, not the mother.

After our stay at the Hotel Tansen, we moved to Hotel Usha Kiran Palace, a government-operated hotel owned by

Maharaja Seindia.

Pradeep would disappear for the day while I stayed in this ornate palace alone until he came home for dinner, I would wander through the empty halls starring at the marble floors or saunter through the gardens smelling each flower as I passed. Jasmine in particular was noticeably fragrant. Peacocks, roaming around the grounds, were my companions. And periodically the managers joined me for lunch but didn't say much.

When I tried to venture out on my own, men appeared from out of nowhere; from doorways, side streets, or from behind trees and followed me, leering, smiling, talking, laughing, inches from my body. It was irritating and scary. I'd walk a block and then have to quickly retreat back to the hotel like a frightened rabbit. This was not what I had expected. This was not good. Once again I felt trapped. Is this the destiny of an Indian wife?

Finally, Pradeep's 16-year-old brother, Sunil, came to the rescue. His English was very good. He was respectful and courteous and offered to escort me everywhere. He showed me museums and historical places. We ate food outside on the streets where we talked and laughed. I didn't know the whereabouts of my husband, but with Sunil, I felt safe and content.

I did ask Pradeep why he left me alone all day and he informed me that he was planning his sister's wedding. Since his father's death and because he was the oldest son in the area, he was responsible for all wedding arrangements. This was an enormous responsibility in the Indian culture.

At least, he could have explained the situation to me at the beginning. I assumed I would be included in this great event and was quite excited with the prospects of experiencing a real Indian wedding, but not having been introduced to Pradeep's mother, I realized I was not accepted as a family member and would not be allowed to attend. Perhaps, his mother would be most upset with Pradeep if she knew of his marriage to a foreigner. I had a fleeting sensation: *perhaps, he already had an Indian wife who he was meeting and who needed to be entertained.* Doubt and disappointment clouded my thoughts.

Sometimes Pradeep and I ate with Rakesh's family, excluding his mother, of course. One night at his brother's house we had a fabulous feast with family and friends. Musicians joined the festivities and played for hours. The women sat on one side of the lawn minding the children and the men were on the other side drinking, smoking, laughing, dancing and having fun. Out of respect for their traditions, I sat with the women quietly nodding my head to the rhythm of the music and watching my husband having a grand old time. Occasionally, he'd wave and smile at me. What I really wanted to do was to dance wildly, drink and sing with the men. Frustrated, I went to bed when the other women did.

Rakesh not only supported the Congress Party, but he was a teacher at the Gwalior Kinder Garten Children's School. One day Rakesh asked if I would be interested in giving the children at his school an English lesson. I was thrilled to be acknowledged and also eager to be of some use. "Of course," I said. "I'd be delighted." The kids were so excited and attentive when I entered the little room. Sitting up straight, cross-legged on the dirt floor, with hands folded on their laps, they were ready to learn. Their bright dark eyes stared at me, eagerly waiting to do whatever I said. In a chorus they sang out the sounds of the English alphabet and repeated after me the simple words which I wrote on the blackboard. (It is very rewarding for a teacher when the students sincerely want to learn.) The children were also eager to teach me a few words in Hindi! *namaste* (hello), *acchaa* (good), *ek* (one).

Another day Pradeep surprised me. He brought me along to sit with a group of his men friends. I could tell they were not pleased, but Pradeep seemed happy I was there. We sat crossed legged in a circle on the ground. Some men were smoking, and some were drinking chai and talking rapidly about serious matters, politics, the economy, and perhaps about me. Of course, I didn't understand a word and Pradeep did not translate. They did smile and nod their heads at me (left to right), and I nodded back respectfully, so perhaps I had earned their approval after all. But I was out with my husband and, for me, that was all that mattered.

After a month of visiting Gwalior and taking side trips to the Taj Mahal, the Red Fort, and other tourist attractions, we needed to head back to New Delhi to catch a plane to Thailand. We arrived in New Delhi just in time for a storm. The wind, dust and rain whipped through every imaginable crack of our hotel room. Dust was in our hair, on our skin, and in our mouths. Again we held on to each other as we experienced another aspect of India.

Storms and heat and crowds aside, India had a charm and spiritual ambiance I couldn't adequately describe. Perhaps it was the constant mystical music and singing, which followed us throughout the day, embracing every inch of our souls, as well as the odors of curry and jasmine permeating the air, that made this country so intriguing to me.

Mother Wouldn't Approve ... Pradeep

PAN AM FLIGHT 001 arrived in New Delhi at four o'clock in the morning on an extremely hot day ... not easy to breathe in the summer's heat wave. We were to meet up with Rakesh, for he had arranged a meeting with Indira Gandhi.

Rakesh, Jane and I arrived at her residence and were greeted cordially by her close associate, Gulam Navi Avad. He led us into a parlor where Mrs. Gandhi welcomed us.

Chai was served and introductions were made.

I introduced my wife, Jane, an American, and told her we are on our honeymoon. For some reason, I needed to tell her I was a permanent resident of the United States and had been living there for almost 10 years. I mentioned that Jane was a daughter of a CIA agent, but not to worry, she was a trustworthy person. We smiled, intended to be taken lightly. Rakesh told her that I owned a world-wide travel company based in Denver, Colorado and that I was in the process of developing an overland passenger transport service. She was impressed and I handed her my business card.

Mrs. Gandhi shared her condolences with Rakesh and me, regarding the death of my father. She wanted us to know how valuable Hari was to her throughout the recent years.

A messenger announced that she had a phone call and at that time, we thanked her and said our good-byes.

We took a cab to New Delhi's railway station in Paharganj to board a train to Gwalior. There was no time to reserve seats for us, so we had to travel in the unreserved coach with our two large suitcases. Traveling with backpacks would have been more practical but it would have been insulting for me to travel that way, especially going home with a Western wife. I needed to have a porter to carry my bags to maintain my status and image. This is a common Indian mentality. The coach was crowded and stuffy and turned out to be an extremely uncomfortable five-hour journey.

When we arrived in Gwalior, I hired a porter to carry our bags to a cab. After a few minutes ride, we reached Hotel Tansen, the second-best hotel in Gwalior and a unit of the Madhya Pradesh Government. Hotel Tansen was fairly clean with a decent size room and was equipped with modern amenities. After a bath and a late breakfast, I had to leave Jane alone so I could walk to my mother's house. It was less than a mile from the hotel. I could not take Jane with me.

Hindu marriages are largely based on "*Kundali* matching" (horoscope matching) and it was grossly ignored by me when I married Jane. Traditional Indian culture, however, considered it a crucial step before making any final commitment to the prospective bride and groom. Although I did not believe in this horoscope matching ritual, my mother did and she would never have allowed her son or daughter to marry without matching the "*Gunas*" (qualities) with their prospective partners. Marriage, in the Hindu community, was considered to be a sacred union in which the couple should not only follow in this life, but in the next seven consecutive lives as well.

It is my belief that nature considers man and woman as a single identity after marriage. As a result, our marriage, our destiny, luck, and fate, influence each other. It can either be created wonderful or can lead to rotten relationship. I did not introduce Jane to my mother because she would have disagreed with my decision. My mother might have created a disturbing scene because my marriage to Jane was performed without *kundali milan*, which, according to my mother's belief, played a vital role in decoding the marriage compatibility of her son and his wife.

After ten days in Gwalior we headed north to Kashmir, the Paradise of Asia. The higher and upper middle classes consider Kashmir a honeymoon destination. I thought Jane and I would enhance our relationship by being somewhere romantic, living on a houseboat with a neat, clean atmosphere. I made a train reservation from Gwalior to Jammu. In Jammu we got on a local tour bus to Srinagar, an eight-hour journey. When we arrived at the West Terminal, we did not have to look very long to rent a houseboat. The agents found us. We chose one that was on Nagin Lake, an offshoot of Dahl Lake, at the foothill of the Zabarwan Mountains. The accommodations were not the best. I'd say a 2-star rating. But the view from our deck was beautiful: magical, romantic, peaceful. The mountains, the lake, and the view of the temples justified our stay. I did not want any disturbances while we were there, so I hired a local security guard with instructions not to allow entry of peddlers trying to sell trinkets. I wanted us to have peace and quiet.

On our arrival, the owner of the houseboat, Abdula, served us chai and in the evening he and his family prepared a Kashmiri vegetarian dinner along with a couple of beers. I asked him to join us for a beer, but he refused. I forgot – Muslims don't drink alcohol. The next day he arranged a sightseeing tour to Gulmarg and Pahalgam. Gulmarg is one of the most popular hill stations in Northern India, boasting of having the highest golf course in the world and the most amazing wildflowers. Pahalgam, known as the "Valley of the Shepherds," is a pilgrimage site for reaching the mountain cave of Lord Shiva. The views of the Himalayas are spectacular. I noticed Jane was happy as we experienced this part of the world.

The following day Jane was invited to visit Abdula's family. His wife and sister were interested to know more about Western women and Jane's experience being married to an Indian man. With their little understanding of the English language, Jane tried to explain with hand and body gestures some of the differences between the two cultures, such as clothing, food, and eating habits. She enjoyed her visit and mentioned the green and white dress Abdula's wife was wearing. I told Abdula about Jane's comment on his wife's dress and asked how I could get her one. "No problem" he said. Next morning Abdul's 18-year old son served us Kashmiri green tea. He also carried a package containing the green and white dress that Abdul's wife had been wearing the day before. It had been washed and pressed and presented to my wife. In an Indian's mind, it may have been a nice gesture but to a Westerner, it was not appropriate. I was upset with Abdula for giving my wife a used dress. He said he had not intended to create an insult in any way.

His son who was mentally disabled took it upon himself to clean the dress and deliver it to Jane as a gift of kindness. In a few days Jane received a new dress from Abdula's family, designed the same as the used one. Everyone was pleased.

Abdula explained that he had consulted medical experts in the mental health field about his son's condition and was told that they could provide treatment for him but that it would cost $460. I thought I should help him out and offered him $500. He accepted the offer and in return wanted to make me half owner of his houseboat. I explained to him my business venture with "Bus Stop Tours" from Frankfurt and after some discussion, we agreed that Srinagar could be part of the route. We both felt this would be a profitable partnership and the next day we went to his lawyer to prepare a legal agreement. I instructed him to carry out all communications for "Bus Stop Tours" with "World Ways Travel" in Denver, Colorado. If all went well, "Bus Stop Tours" would be a subsidiary of "World Ways Travel Company."

At this time, Jane was not feeling well; lacking energy and looking noticeably thin. She wanted to continue with our travels and move on to our next destination: Bangkok, Thailand.

Bliss On the Beach ... Jane

BANGKOK WAS ALIVE WITH color and excitement. We gazed upon the Golden Buddha, absorbing the feeling of ancient spiritually. We took a traditional long-tail boat with a driver who paddled us along the canal of the Damnoen Saduak floating market, where we viewed boats, piled high with fresh vegetables, tropical fruits, handbags, souvenirs, coconut milk, and bright colored flowers. Everyone was bargaining, yelling out prices of their offerings. The atmosphere was friendly, chaotic and festive. The food and smells stimulated the senses; all strange and enticing.

We stayed in a comfortable hotel occupied by other young travelers. The owner of the hotel suggested we take a boat to the island of Koh Sumui. After a few days of sightseeing in Bangkok, we traveled by bus to a little village where we boarded a small ferry to the island. Here we hopped into a jeep and were driven along a narrow dirt road to a beach with little huts along the shore. One was for us. Our spot on the beach was beautiful. We could step out of our hut onto the white sand and walk a few feet to the aqua-colored tranquil water. We ate, drank, smoked hash, and made love. I chose to ignore all the previous mishaps of our trip. I decided to get stoned and just float through this leg of our "honeymoon." Everything was perfect.

I figured when we returned to the States I would have to make some choices. But, spending these blissful days together high on hash made me feel we would be alright.

Bliss On the Beach ... Pradeep

WE ARRIVED IN BANGKOK early in the morning and wanted to check into a hotel as soon as possible. The tourist office at the airport suggested a few hotels in the middle of Bangkok on Rama Road. We checked into Hotel Atlantic, located in an old building, decently man- aged by an elderly German fellow. It so happened that he, in his younger years, had been secretary to the then Maharaja Udaipur, Rajastan.

The manager gave us good tourist information suggesting popular places to visit and a list of fine Thai vegetarian restaurants.

He understood the nature of our trip and strongly recommended visiting Koh Sumui island; an island with silver sandy beaches, a perfect place for a honeymoon couple.

After we settled into our room, we joined him for coffee before going on a local sightseeing trip. In three days he would arrange our bus journey with reserved seats to Surat Thani where we would board a ferry to Koh Sumui.

When we arrived at the ferry terminal, we had to wait three hours until the ticket office opened. A roadside cafe served breakfast, so we had plenty of time to eat something. However, all they served was fish and rice. I don't eat fish. It was difficult to get a vegetarian breakfast. I ate rice. Jane was dissatisfied with their cooking style, so she remained with no breakfast.

On the ferry we befriended a young Thai woman by the name of Lily. She suggested a place to stay on a beach in straw huts. She happened to be a cook at the restaurant next to the huts and we would be able to have the meals of our choice. Lily arranged our accommodations and proceeded to fix us a well-prepared vegetarian hot lunch. It was delicious! Jane and I appreciated the warm sand and beautiful beach. These were the most relaxing days since India.

Instead of staying for the three days as planned, we extended our stay for another week. We hired a jeep to take us around the island, exploring the jungles and mountainous areas. Finding places to eat and drink while smoking Thai grass made it a perfect all-day adventure. It was peaceful. We developed more self-confidence toward each other. This would help us to lead our life in an appropriate direction, in a healthy way. Our future looked positive. We ate well thanks to Lily, and we enjoyed the laid-back atmosphere of the island.

Our time was running out, and we needed to move on to our next destination. I wanted to catch a bus from Surat Thani to Pattaya Beach, but Jane was against it for two reasons: the beach town was known for its prostitutes, and she felt unwell.

Hong Kong ... Jane

WHEN FLYING INTO HONG Kong, I remember flying over a body of water between two land masses. It looked as though we would land smack into the water. Fortunately, the pilot had everything under control, and we reached the runway safely.

Hong Kong was crowded, mega-crowded. As we wandered through the city, we literally walked touching the people next to us, moving along shoulder to shoulder and nose to back of head. Here people walked tightly in an orderly manner, whereas in India, the walking pattern seemed chaotic and scrambled.

Our hotel room was on the 14th floor inside a mall with an Indian restaurant on the floor above us. The smells were delightful. However, the room was minuscule, without windows. Once again for me claustrophobic, as I was on the train in India. What if there were a fire? I didn't feel comfortable at all. Luckily, we stayed there only to sleep.

I was told that Hong Kong was a great place to buy prescription eyeglasses. One day, we set out to find an optometrist to fit me with a new pair. In less than a week my glasses were ready and cost only thirty dollars compared to two hundred dollars for my prescription in the States.

One evening, we left the hotel in search of an authentic local Chinese restaurant. After a half-hour walk, we came across a section of the city with no neon lights or tall buildings. It was quieter and there were not a million people crushed together. We found a simple small restaurant: no decorations on the walls, just worn, well-used tables and chairs. The menu was written in Chinese with no English translation. The other customers, all Chinese, just stared at us. We obviously didn't fit in. We were an unusual looking couple and they seemed genuinely curious why we had stumbled into their restaurant. When we pointed to items on the menu, our fellow diners would nod in approval with a smile, or shake their heads making a frown, chatting amongst themselves discussing our decisions. We enjoyed our evening tremendously even though we hadn't a clue what we ordered or ate!

Another day I decided to take a bus to the border of Communist China. Tourists couldn't walk over to the other side, of course, but I wanted to see something different from the hustle and bustle of city life. The countryside was filled with little huts scattered up the hillside. It was amazing to see men and women coming out of their shacks walking down the hill to catch the bus or train to go to work. They were dressed immaculately: make-up, shiny shoes, well groomed, western styled suits, skirts, high heels, ready for another workday in the city. The border itself wasn't that exciting, but the views from the bus were.

Pradeep was annoyed with me for going off like that, especially because I disagreed with him. That night while in bed in the windowless room of the hotel, I thought he leaned over to me and whispered in my ear, "You know, you're not going to live long. Someone is going to kill you, but it won't be me!" For several moments I stopped breathing. What was he talking about? I must have been having a nightmare or was he talking in his sleep? Did he really say this or was I imagining it? Needless to say, I stayed awake all night just in case I had to defend myself.

In the morning, he woke up cheerful, as if nothing out of the ordinary had happened. I hadn't slept at all and moved around him cautiously. I must have been dreaming.

The day was beautiful and he talked about taking a ferry to explore the other side of the harbor. I watched him carefully, on guard. He approached me affectionately and took my hand as we walked toward the dock. I was confused.

We watched families as they sold their fish, wares and food to people on the docks. Hundreds of junks (boats) were either docked or sailing in the harbor.

We talked and laughed as we explored our surroundings. The fears of the night before vanished.

Our next stop was Tokyo. Soon we'd be in Honolulu, Hawaii where we would be relaxing on the sandy beaches in the Hawaiian Islands. I just wished I felt better.

I had lost a lot of weight. I looked emaciated. I had little energy. Doubts about our relationship and what the future had in store plagued me. I, also, wondered about the fire and robbery back in Denver and if the situation had been solved.

Hong Kong ... Pradeep

JANE WAS NOT COMFORTABLE on the short flight from Bangkok to Hong Kong. Her breakfast did not settle well. We arrived at nine in the morning and she seemed to be even more tired and catching some illness. Perhaps she had gotten something from a mosquito bite in Thailand.

I had a recommendation to stay at the Chung Kin Guest House on Nathan Road next to the Sheraton Hotel. At the guest house we could have breakfast to satisfy our hunger. It was owned and operated by an Indian Sikh and I knew we would be served good vegetarian food throughout our six day stay. Our accommodations were unsatisfactory, how- ever, but the food served in the restaurant on the floor above us justified the inconvenience of our room.

During the day we explored Hong Kong with minimum conversation between us. I frequently asked Jane how her health was and most of the time I received an unsatisfactory answer from her. Her health was a growing concern; she was losing weight. I tried to understand her feelings but she seemed to ignore anything I said or did to help her. At one point, I thought she was playing games with me.

Sleep at night was less than perfect. After breakfast one day, trying to please her, I gave her my credit card so she could buy what- ever she wanted in the Arcade. But she was not interested in that either.

Some strange feeling started entering my mind. She repeatedly told me how she felt about not meeting my mother and I wondered if this was still a problem. I tried to explain the situation with my family and Hindu culture, but it was beyond her capability to understand the circumstances that I had been going through with my immediate family members, my mother in particular.

We continued to sightsee with little conversation. This was not our usual manner and I was hoping it was a temporary problem which would be resolved soon.

The next day we started walking towards the ghetto area of the city just to get away from the crowds and flashy scenery of downtown Hong Kong. I thought it might help change our thoughts, but it was not a great help.

Jane then, wanted to take a bus to the border town of Macau which bordered Communist China. I wanted to avoid going anywhere near the Chinese border because I knew the British Intelligence Service would be keeping an eye on foreign visitors. I could not convince her not to go and we had a stupid argument over it. I reluctantly let her go on the half-day bus tour and hoped she would feel better having her personal freedom. When she returned, however, she still remained quiet.

The next day, we went to the airport to catch a flight to Honolulu. We could not find anything to talk about. A very negative couple. "No" was a frequent word used between us. Our documents were in order so we went through customs without problems. We had an hour before the plane left and I asked Jane if she wanted a coffee. "No" was her reply. I didn't know how to get her mind back to normal. After I drank my delicious cup of coffee, I asked her if she was ready to board the plane. She said "Yes!"

We boarded Pan Am Flight 001, #747 aircraft with capacity of five hundred passengers but it was only half full. I let Jane have my window seat, so she could look out the window and enjoy the scenery. I took the aisle seat so I could watch TV. Normally, we would hold each other's hand during takeoff and landing, but not this time.

When the aircraft reached cruising speed, we were allowed to unfasten our seat belts. A young man walked by and quietly asked if I smoked. I said, "Yes" and joined him in the back of the plane's smoking section. He was a young G.I. in the U.S. Army having served in South Korea. We shared stories, smoked his two joints and enjoyed the high feelings above the clouds. I had with me a nut bolt smoking pipe but nothing to smoke. He said he had a similar pipe and had some hash in his check-in luggage and would be happy to give me some. Then, given the stress I felt with Jane, I could have a few hits before I reached Honolulu.

Our flight stopped at the airport in Tokyo, where we were given a boarding pass and allowed to stay in the transient lounge until we were ready to board our next plane. Within an hour, the G.I. made his way to the EXIT door and handed over some hash which he had placed in a Marlboro cigarette pack. Jane was unaware of my smoking. I wonder if she was curious as to why I had such a big smile on my face. When the plane took off for Honolulu, Jane took my hand.

As soon as the plane leveled off, I needed to find a discreet place to fill my hash pipe. The only place to support my secret deed was the toilet. When my mission was accomplished, I returned to my seat next to Jane just in time for lunch. After which, I respectfully asked the stewardess if I could sit in a vacant seat in the back where the smoking section was. She said there was no problem. I showed Jane my pipe. She wasn't interested and told me to be careful. I jokingly said, "Don't worry! There are no cops around!" With a smile, I left for the back of the plane, took a seat, ordered a Budweiser and fired up my pipe. What a lovely experience, I thought, being high in the sky and traveling with a beautiful American girl who was my wife. I was enjoying my thoughts when the stewardess stopped and asked me,

"Sir, what are you smoking?"

"It's a kind of Indian tobacco" I proclaimed with great authority.

"You are not supposed to smoke that stuff on the plane!" she scolded.

Smugly, I said, "What is the problem? That man in front of me is smoking a cigar and this is the smoking section." She gave me a strange look and walked away toward the pilot's cabin. Shortly thereafter, the Head Flight Attendant passed by, looked at me and continued on. By the time I finished my pipe, we were ready to land. I joined Jane, took her hand, and prepared for landing, arriving in beautiful Hawaii for the last leg of our honeymoon.

Wait For Me ... Jane, July 1979

FROM TOKYO, WE WOULD fly to Honolulu, spend time on the beach, relax and enjoy the last portion of our trip and then continue on to San Francisco. What was going to happen after our return, I did not know. I worried about my future with Pradeep. I didn't understand him. His behavior during the trip baffled me and he had a lot of explaining to do concerning his travel agency.

When we landed in Honolulu, I suddenly realized we would be going through customs here, not in San Francisco. I prayed everything would go smoothly. We waited in the long line, showed our passports, and our bags were searched. Then, the worst happened. We were asked to step aside and were escorted to a private room.

Our bags were searched again. In Pradeep's luggage, the security guard found a hash pipe which contained a minuscule amount of residue. I assumed the hash pipe was the excuse the security guards needed to search him more thoroughly. A women officer requested I come with her into the ladies bathroom where she could search me, too. I was furious! I told her not to touch me, that I had nothing on me or in me. She knew that and noticing I didn't look well, gently ushered me back to the waiting area.

I felt weak, scared and disgusted. Pradeep tried to lift my spirits with his usual panache, by saying it was just a misunderstanding and he would straighten everything out. About an hour later, the Honolulu Police came with a warrant from Denver County for his arrest for felony and arson. The police informed us that Pradeep would have to stay in Honolulu in a detention center for several days, then he would be flown to Denver.

I did expect a possible encounter with the authorities when we got back to Denver, but not an arrest at the airport here in Honolulu. Before we left San Francisco, the Denver police had told Pradeep he was free to leave the country.

Are you going to take me too?" I asked.

"No, it is just Pradeep we want," The policeman replied. What was I to do now? Alone?

Pradeep gave me the money he had in his pocket, five hundred dollars. He put his arms around me and reassured me that everything would be alright. With the police by his side, he departed with a lilt in his step and a smile on his face. What an exit!

People stared and whispered amongst themselves. It was late at night and the airport emptied out quickly. I found myself sitting on a bench with just our luggage. No one asked if I needed help or if I was OK.

I didn't know what to do. I finally spotted a cleaning lady and asked if there was someone who could help me get to a hotel. She pointed to the "Quick Book a Hotel Box:" a machine in which I had to press a button next to the hotel I wanted. I didn't know what I wanted. There were so many hotels to choose from that I became confused. I felt dizzy, feverish, thirsty. I pulled myself together and clicked on a button, any button. It did not matter. Then pressed another button that beckoned a taxi. A sense of numbness came over me and in a trance I made it to the hotel. I proceeded to compulsively take four showers and two baths. I cried uncontrollably for what seemed like hours. After calming down, I called my brother in Fremont to let him know what had happened.

"I know," he said

"What do you mean, you know?" I cried.

He explained that the story of the travel agent fleeing with his clients' money had been national news: headlines in the newspapers, on TV and on radio stations. I was shocked! He was relieved to know I was safe and told me to get the next flight back to San Francisco. He'd be there to pick me up.

The next morning I flew out of Honolulu still confused, weak and angry.

Paul met me at the airport, and brought me back to his house where I collapsed on his living room floor.

34

Wait For Me ... Pradeep, July 1979

I WAS LOOKING FORWARD TO spending the remainder of our honeymoon in Honolulu, hoping that Jane and I could discuss our differences and gain an understanding and compassion for each other. This was "paradise," after all! When we disembarked, I noticed a couple of security guards following us, but I ignored them. At customs, our luggage was searched and then we were asked to follow an airline security officer to another room. I was searched. After ten minutes of "pat down," they found my empty uncleaned hash pipe. It took another ten minutes for them to scratch out all the blackish ash residue from the pipe.

They decided the substance was an opiate, even though just a small amount. I had to sign some papers to verify that the pipe belonged to me and the substance found also belonged to me.

While all this was taking place, the immigration officials were apparently informed that I had an arrest warrant issued by the Denver Police Department charging me with conspiracy to commit arson with an added charge of theft over $200,000. I was taken into custody.

I remained calm, reassuring Jane that all would be just fine. After a hug and endearing words of goodbye, I was escorted to a police car and driven to a detention center. The center was a well secured building with a few guards on duty. Lunch and dinner were served in a dining hall big enough for twenty inmates, but we were only half this number.

I spent five days in the detention center with a few other "criminals." Two of the men, one from Texas and one from Washington State, were fighting extradition for theft and similar charges. The Honolulu Police department came to me and gave me a choice either to challenge extradition or waive my rights. I chose to waive my rights. Based on the waiver, a Denver Police Officer showed up six days later and showed me the legal arrest warrant. "You will be in my custody, and we will fly to Denver in the afternoon."

When police had separated me from Jane, I thought, "Never leave a true relationship for a few faults. Nobody is perfect and nobody is totally correct. In the end, affection is always greater than perfection."

She knew that my stories were beyond amazing and only equal to the warmth in my heart toward her. We had previously exchanged a lot of valuable information regarding life, marriage, religion, and karma. We had shared the love of American Jazz, food and dancing. What a short, but great time we had had together. Jane considered me "extremely friendly and fascinating." She had a lot of questions regarding life's mysteries and she thought I could help answer them for her and with her.

My happiness, however, depended not only with me but

on Jane, also. We planned to walk together but it was hard for her to march to my "drumbeat."

As I sat on the plane, flying to Denver, I explored ideas and thoughts concerning problems of our existence. I replayed the events that took place before Jane and I left on our trip. I welcomed thoughts from all directions; to understand the nature of women, the identities of the people I trusted. I delved deeper into my consciousness exploring the multicellular human organisms existing within my mind.

I divided women into two categories: Number one is "herself" which represents the woman as her physical self, her mental health and her social surroundings. Number two is "self-realization" which represents the woman as ethically good, morally sound, and spiritually advanced. I am conscious and aware of the nature of Jane's identity and individuality. Our physical being was dissolved by the powerful influence of the changing world of human beings. Almost everything in Nature changes with Time but our identity and individuality remain the same during our life's journey.

In my heart, I wanted to say three words to Jane: "Wait for me!"

"The Nature and Origin of Justice"

They say to do injustice is, by nature, good; to suffer injustice, evil; but that the evil is greater than the good. And so when men have both done and suffered injustice and have had experience of both, not being able to avoid the one and obtain the other, they think that they had better agree among themselves to have neither; hence there arise laws and mutual covenants; and that which is ordained by law is termed by them lawful and just. This they affirm to be the origin and nature of justice; - it is a mean or compromise between the best of all, which is to do injustice and not be punished, and the worst of all, is to suffer injustice without the power of retaliation; and justice, being at the middle point between the two, is tolerated not as good, but as the lesser evil, and honored by reason of the inability of men to do justice. For no man who is worthy to be called a man would ever submit to such an agreement if he were able to resist; he would be mad if he did.

Plato

PART FOUR ✵ DECEPTION

Quarantined ... Jane

I HAD NO APPETITE, MY clothes dangled from my limbs and I itched all over. After a few days of rest at my brother's, I drove myself to the Oakland Hospital to seek some medical advice. The doctors could find nothing wrong with me; the blood work, normal. "Perhaps, it was malaria," they offered, "but you would have to wait a longer period of time before the results showed up in a blood test." I was sent home. Barely able to move and anxious for a more definitive diagnosis, I booked a flight back to the East Coast to see my doctor on Martha's Vineyard.

On the flight home, I sat with a young man who had a cast on his leg.

His leg itched terribly, which put him in a crazy state of mind. I also itched all over and was miserable. Needless to say, the two of us spent the entire trip scratching, complaining and laughing at our comical situation.

Before I left San Francisco, I had called Eleanor, my friend who helped plan my wedding, and explained what had happened: the honeymoon, the money, the arrest. I was not surprised when she told me she already knew about Pradeep's arrest for she had heard it on the radio and on TV.

Eleanor invited me to stay at her house in West Tisbury on Flat Point Farm with her husband, Rick, and their two-year-old daughter, Sarah.

After I arrived and had settled in, I went directly to my doctor's office in Vineyard Haven. I was pale, underweight, and my skin was black and blue from my scratching. The nurse took one look at me and asked if I had always had yellow eyes. That was it! At last a diagnosis: Hepatitis A. Highly contagious. No cure: just rest and fluids.

Before I moved to California in 1971, I had lived in a tent on Flat Point Farm in exchange for weeding the garden for Eleanor's father, Arnold. After I had left the Vineyard, Eleanor decided to join me in California for six months to experience life on the West Coast. Sunny California apparently did not suit her (a waitressing job probably didn't help) because she decided to return to Martha's Vineyard, get married, and have a baby instead.

The farm included the family farmhouse, four or five cottages, a barn and a couple of sheds.

My being on the farm where many people lived caused quite a commotion, because of Hep. A being extremely contagious.

I'd been coming to the Vineyard for summers since I was nineteen and for me to recuperate here felt like the right place to be. Not everyone felt that way. Each person I had had contact with or who was living on the farm had to get a gamma- globulin shot to protect them from getting Hepatitis A. It wouldn't have been so bad if the shot was given in the arm, but this particular injection was administered in the buttocks. They were not a happy lot, especially little Sarah. She was still crying when she returned home from the doctor's.

Because so many people were getting Hepatitis shots all at once, it looked as though there was an epidemic on the Island.

"Outbreak of Hepatitis," was the headline splashed on the front page of the *Vineyard Gazette*, the local newspaper. The health inspector phoned Eleanor's house and personally ordered me quarantined on the farm for a month. And, he made it quite clear, I was not allowed to go to the West Tisbury Agricultural Fair which opened in a week, the "must go to social event" of the entire summer!

Accepting my fate, I recuperated quietly on this beautiful farm surrounded by friends who eventually forgave me for all the discomfort they had endured. Drinking frappes and eating azuki beans helped me gain weight and heal my liver.

At the end of September, I felt well enough to fly to Colorado to see Pradeep at the Denver County Jail.

Denver County Jail ... Pradeep, July, 1979

SECURITY GUARDS SEARCHED MY bags and handed me forms to fill out:

Where was I born? India
What was my religion? Hindu
What kind of food did I eat? Vegetarian
Take any medication? No.
Etc.

After all the paperwork had been completed, an officer escorted me to an eight-by-twelve-foot cell furnished with a bunk bed where I joined one other man. I was given a bed sheet, blanket, pillowcase, pillow, and two orange jumpsuits. The uniforms had my identification number stitched on my pocket, #369852.

Two three story buildings stood on the property. Each floor was given a letter, A, B, C, and so on. I was placed in the second building on the first floor, Floor D, and put into cell 18. It was a custom to attach a name to the letter, so I became known as "Dog 18"; another inmate on Floor F was "Fox 15," another on Floor B was "Badger 7." I chose to be optimistic.

On the third day, a police officer escorted me to the Denver Metropolitan Magistrate Court for a preliminary hearing to face charges of fourteen counts of theft, two counts of arson and conspiracy to commit arson. A public defender was appointed. This is when I had the right to plead guilty or not guilty. I pleaded NOT GUILTY.

The public defender asked the court to consider reducing the bail bond from $250,000 to a more reasonable amount.

The Magistrate was reluctant to agree and said, "This young man has more than a quarter of a million dollars in his possession and he just returned from a $100,000 honey- moon. It's difficult for me to think of changing his bail bond. After a short argument, the PD convinced the Magistrate to reduce the bail to $70,000 for both cases, $20,000 for arson, $50,000 for theft.

When I first arrived at the Denver County Jail as a trial detainee, to my surprise, I met Max who had worked for me at World Ways Travel. Max said Greg had informed Immigration Officials that he was not living with his U.S. citizen wife and had married her simply to obtain his permanent resident's status. He was accused of immigration fraud and was awaiting deportation to Australia.

Max said he had served all the customers of World Ways Travel and money had been refunded to all, except, for four people which amounted to, only $1750. This, I felt, was a defect on my side. He had heard that, before the fire at the agency, Greg had hired a cab and made a deal with the driver to wait outside my apartment until I arrived. The cab driver noticed he had a gun and ordered him out of the car. The driver then called the police. They found Greg boarding a bus and arrested him for carrying a concealed weapon. Greg was then taken to the police station where the gun was confiscated, and he was released. I wish I had known this before we went to the mountains together.

He also said that Greg had been writing checks to himself for a total of one thousand dollars. He and Janet began paying bills to creditors before the payment was due. With me taking money out for my trip, the bank account had dwindled, leaving little money left to manage the business.

I really thought all would work out. I hadn't counted on my employees taking matters into their own hands.

Several months went by and not a single person who knew me, my friends, my wife, two cousins, employees, Scout, and in short, my entire world of friends, showed up with the bail money. They turned out to be afraid to acknowledge me.

Eventually, I was handed more than one hundred papers, including a charge sheet which explained why I had been arrested. The investigation report conducted by the Denver Police Department confirmed charging me with fourteen counts of theft, two counts of arson, and conspiracy to commit arson.

Included in those papers was Greg's false statement of me hiring two black men to rob and set fire to my business. He even had airline tickets to prove it. He had access to blank airline tickets and could have easily forged them himself. I was convinced Greg had made a deal with the district attorney to drop his gun charges and him from being a possible suspect, in return for supplying him with information against me. Based on Greg's false information an arrest warrant had been issued by the Denver authorities. It was an unusual "red corner" warrant through the U.S. State Department to arrest me from anywhere in the world. The warrant was sent to MI6, Scotland Yard of U.K., Interpol of France, Germany, India, and many more countries and this caught the eye of the media, which reflected my guilt. In Honolulu they found a search warrant from the Denver Police Department. I didn't know what it was for. I thought that whatever happened in Denver would be resolved in my absence. Before Jane and I left for London I was told the investigation would continue but I was free to go on my normal business trip as well as my honeymoon. A new office for the agency was in operation and my presence was not needed at that time.

I was allowed one phone call. I called a famous criminal lawyer by the name of Charles Jacobs. He was unavailable and sent his junior attorney, Don Gordon, to represent me. Mr. Gordon convinced me he could win the case, but his retainer fee was quite high. He took it upon himself to contact my list of people who might be able to raise the funds needed for the fee.

He contacted many friends, including Jane. Most people were surprised about the charges and wanted to help, but the help was not received in time. Finally, Dan, who owed me $1,720, sent a cashier's check. With this money, I hired another criminal lawyer, Sam Harris. A tenor was signed that he would take only the arson case. The theft case was referred to a public defender.

Media was all over this story. In my absence, my name was blasted all over every newspaper in the United States with headlines like:

INDIAN NATIONAL ARRESTED FOR ARSON AND THEFT DEFRAUDING MANY AIRLINES AND SEVERAL CUSTOMERS.

I wrote to University National Bank and asked them to send my canceled checks in order to reestablish my account and bookkeeping. When I received them, I noticed a number of suspicious items: Greg's unauthorized signature on several checks amounting to almost $1,000 and bills payed before due date by Janet and Greg. I was beginning to suspect a conspiracy to embezzle money from several airlines controlled by American Traffic Conference. That plus the fact that I was out of town traveling with my wife, and that there were tickets missing, plus an arson investigation that was still in process, left me with a lot deal with.

I often questioned how the U.S. government determined what was and was not legal in the travel world. I believed that selling reduced airline tickets led to increased numbers of travelers and benefited all airlines. Was that actually illegal? Apparently, it was in my case, because I neglected to fill out the proper papers. That was another strike against me. The attorney felt doubtful toward me.

"It was not like that at all!" I tried to explain, but I was ignored.

During my absence my bank account was seized, therefore accounts receivable which amounted to $100,000 could not be deposited into my business account and my colleagues couldn't run the business without old records, and the business came to an abrupt halt. I was hoping that the new office could reestablish itself with new records and that the reports would soon be released by the fire department. I attempted to reestablish my business accounts through the bank, but it became impossible to conduct business transactions while behind prison walls.

I wrote to my family in India along with other friends who were my "well-wishers" that I was in police custody under false charges. As soon as my brother Rakesh heard of this, he rushed to New Delhi to inform Mrs. Gandhi that his brother Pradeep had been arrested by US authorities and framed with false charges. He reminded her of Pradeep's visit with his wife two months earlier. She indeed remembered.

Rakesh was the leader of the Young Wing of the Indian National Congress Party and knew that she should be aware of Pradeep's arrest in the US. Next day, a delegate of the ruling Congress Party went to the US Embassy in New Delhi and demanded the release of Pradeep from the Denver County Jail with immediate effect.

Rakesh wrote to tell me how protesters held posters with my picture on them outside the US Embassy threatening the US Ambassador to have me released or they will burn the Embassy down!

My case went to the Minister of Foreign Affairs of India who instructed the Indian Embassy in Washington, D.C. to secure my release and to report on my well-being. From there, a Consulate General of India in San Francisco was appointed to physically visit me and make a report.

The Denver District Judge, Edward Taylor, was flooded with letters from India which spoke favorably of me.

After a week in the county jail, I had felt abandoned and rejected by my friends. I was depressed. The diet at the jail consisted mostly of meat and I didn't eat meat. Therefore, I ate bread, cottage cheese and occasionally fruit, but it wasn't a balanced diet. Now I was the one losing weight and not feeling well.

The jail doctor suggested a special vegetarian diet, but to the cooks, that meant simply taking the meat off the plate. They didn't understand that my religious vegetarian diet needed to be cooked in a "pure vegetarian manner"; no meat-based sauces; utensils and cutting boards needed to be used only for vegetables.

I filed a complaint which read:

> *"The applicant, at the time of entry into the Denver County Jail, notified the Jail Authorities that he was born in India, and that his 5000 year-old religion was well known and rooted in Sanatan Dharma. Also, he himself, registered in the city and county of Denver, State of Colorado, under title "International Society of Govinda People." In addition, he is a life member of International Society of Krishna Consciousness." Since birth he was raised by a strict vegetarian Brahmin family, i.e. meat, fish, eggs, poultry cannot be consumed by him. Finally, three meals in 24 hours would be required by him."*

I asked Sam Harris to file a motion in Denver District Court to provide vegetarian meals. I did win this lawsuit on November 25, 1979; however, it was not implemented. I then had to file contempt of court order against the Denver County Jail Administration. I continued on a limited diet which resulted in my losing my health.

At the same time, I was disturbed that mail was opened and read before delivering it to the inmates and I filed a complaint about that, too. Much to my astonishment, the postal authorities took this matter very seriously and issued necessary instruction to the concerning jail authorities to right that wrong. They said it was an unfair, and an unethical tactic and changed the rules to comply with my complaint.

It seemed that most of my time in jail, I was fighting for my fundamental rights (food being my main priority), dealing with doctors, trying to communicate with the outside world, and reading law books in the library. I needed to learn how to defend my Constitutional rights which were guaranteed under the 14th amendment, known as Due Process of Law and defined as: *a fundamental, constitutional guarantee that all legal proceedings will be fair and that one will be given notice of the proceedings and an opportunity to be heard before the government acts to take away one's life, liberty, or property. Also, a constitutional guarantee that a law shall not be unreasonable, arbitrary, or capricious.*

Being a non-citizen, the immigration Department had issued a detainer to determine if I was subject to deportation after the court case was finalized. Anxiety nipped away at my brain.

Thoughts of the fire, robbery, and arrest raced around in my head, replaying over and over again causing a sense of madness to creep over me. But I knew I had to keep focused to survive this ordeal. I was alone, totally helpless.

37

The Visit ... Jane, September 1979

OH, THE DRAMA ... the heartache ... the anguish! This man, sitting in the county jail, confused me, challenged me. I wanted to hold and protect him, but, in all truth, I didn't know who he was, at this point, nor trust him. I wanted to believe he was innocent. But as far as everybody knew, he was already guilty, accused of robbing money from his clients and setting fire to his own business. No proof of his guilt had yet surfaced that I knew of, but he was a minority, a man from India; what chance did he have? HE WAS GOING TO PRISON! Perhaps he would be deported and if deported would not be eligible for entry into the USA for another 7 years.

My thoughts of despair:

> *If I don't divorce him, am I going to follow him to India and live there for seven years? What if he is guilty? What if he is lying? What if he goes to prison in India? What if I'm not allowed to leave India? I would probably never be able to get a*

> *divorce. Divorcing him now will give him the freedom to start a new life and I will be able to move on with my own life.*

Walking into this concrete building sent chills up my spine. I followed the guard along an empty cold grey corridor, our steps echoing in my ears. He opened several huge thick iron doors, slamming each behind us. I shivered. He led me to a small, cell-like room with a chair and a counter that was connected to another counter divided by a security window. A telephone sat on both counters and this was how Pradeep and I were to communicate. He strutted in with a huge grin on his face, sat down and lifted the receiver.

He told me he was pleased to see me and that he remained optimistic. But seeing him in his orange suit disturbed me. If he was depressed or scared, he did not show it. He had lost weight and it was heartbreaking to see him like that. I was determined to focus on doing as much to help him as I could while in Denver. After all, I was still his wife and sincerely cared for his well-being.

He mentioned he was writing letters to India in order to get help from the authorities and was doing everything he could to get answers and help for his case. To me, however, if he hadn't been so careless, naive or reckless, none of this would have happened. He had explained the meaning of karma to me when we first met. I hated to admit it, but I put all of his fiascoes into the "Ignorant Karma" category.

After I spoke with him, I met with a Public Defender and together we searched for Pradeep's friends who might be able to help in the investigation. These were the people who had worked with him, socialized with him, prayed with him at the Krishna Temple and wished us love and happiness on our wedding day; yet no one could be found. It was as if they had never existed. I felt as if the whole situation was a conspiracy, a set up against him. But, why?

If his colleagues were innocent, why did they disappear? Pradeep had a project and I could not help him. I had to let him go and start my life anew. This whole outcome disturbed me. I sincerely wanted our life to go as planned, but it hadn't.

When I visited him the second time, a few days later, I was escorted to a larger room with chairs and tables, no window separating us this time, but a guard stood at the door. I had nothing positive to tell Pradeep and finding words to express what I was feeling was difficult. No matter how dismal his future looked, he still felt optimistic.

During our meeting, Pradeep and I were not allowed to touch each other, but when it was time to leave, I could not resist the impulse to feel his embrace once again. We hugged, holding on as if it were the last time.

The guard yelled at us, "No Touching!"

Our embrace was brief, but at least we parted with a touch of caring and hope. Hope that both of us would be okay.

I stood outside the prison wall and cried. I cried for him. I cried for myself. My dreams had been shattered. I was angry with him because he ruined our plans of being together.

I left Denver heartbroken.

By the time I reached Martha's Vineyard, I had made my decision.

Plea Bargain … Pradeep, February, 1980

ARREST AND INCARCERATION IN Denver County Jail was harder for me than being married. Under the weight of distant living, shame and mutual misunderstanding, I succumbed to the fact that my marriage to Jane might fall apart. An inmate in Honolulu said, "Ninety-nine percent of American White women married to Asian men walk away due to the man's arrest. Even if the marriage survives the prison sentence, it would be difficult to maintain a healthy relationship with her." I thought he was joking, and I took it lightly.

Her visit lifted my spirits, but her letters, there must have been two dozen, implied both positive and negative feelings. I never felt anything negative toward her or our marriage, because on March 10, 1979, our wedding day, while taking seven irreversible circles, three promises were made by me:

1. I will arrange your financial or other necessary requirements;

2. I will protect you from any life's danger (security);

3. I will never leave you or walk away from you until death.

After Jane first filed for divorce in Alameda County Superior Court, I denied the marriage per American Laws. I wrote to the court that this wedding was carried out according to Hindu Marriage Laws and divorce did not exist.

I explained to the court, "As I understand in your terms, marriage is based on a contract. That contract is based on an agreement and in the English dictionary, 'agreement' has an opposite word, 'disagreement'. Whereas, Hindus have never created an opposite word for 'agreement' in relationship to Marriage (*vivah*) which is a lifetime commitment. Therefore, the court should not interfere in this case."

The case was referred to ACLU (American Civil Liberty Union) for their legal opinion.

At the end in 1981, divorce was granted based on exparte decision.

With my own reasoning, it was best just to say I was not married. That way I would not break my Hindu religious law. I did not sign the divorce papers.

At this time, I was considerably ill. The doctors evaluated my illness to lack of protein. A high protein diet with lots of fruits and vegetables was suggested as well as supplemental medication. My health worsened and finally, I was diagnosed with a mild case of TB. More medication was prescribed, and eventually I got better.

A few days after six months without any trial, the Denver District Attorney's Office sent a message through the staff nurse, urging me to accept a plea bargain with the District Attorney's Office and plead guilty to minimum charges and in turn, I would get jail time credit. It was the only way for me to survive, to get out of there and improve my lost health. A few days later, I received a letter from the District Attorney's Office which read:

> "Your client will plead guilty before Judge Edward Taylor in case No. 79-CR-1433 to the principal count herein, which is a Class 4 felony, and to an added count of theft as per the enclosed i.e. count 2 of 1433. Additionally, at the time of sentencing I will recommend to the court that the sentence be within the presumptive guidelines under the most recently enacted sentencing statute and that "no extraordinary circumstances" exists which would warrant sentencing beyond those guidelines."

My understanding of a plea bargain was to allow the defendant to plead guilty of charge in exchange for an agreement with the prosecutor to drop one or more charges to lessen the sentence.

All along I was aware of my constitutional rights for a "speedy trial." It should take place within 180 days. After 180 days had passed without a trial, I lost hope. At this time, I would do anything to get me out of jail, so I could move on to make things right again. If I agreed to the plea bargain, this arrangement could be made quickly, and I would have a lesser sentence.

I never imagined it would come down to this; that one

day, I would have to make a decision whether I should plead guilty to something I didn't do.

On February 7, 1980, I agreed to do so: plead guilty to arson, a Class 4 felony, and an added count of theft, two hundred dollars but not more than ten thousand dollars, both crimes arising from the same transaction, also a Class 4 felony (minimum of 2 years, a maximum of 5) which would warrant sentencing beyond the guidelines set under the newly acted Gorsuch Bill. No extraordinary circumstances would exist.

I was on a lot of medication I didn't know if I would live or die. I was desperate, but I did know, I WAS NOT GUILTY! If I agreed to the plea bargain, I would get out of jail sooner which meant I could gain back my lost health. It was a serious decision to choose between freedom and death. Under normal conditions, I would never, never, never agree to plead guilty. Harris, my lawyer taking the arson case, egged me on to say "Yes, Yes, Yes," and I said "Yes." With a guilty plea, it would be understood that I would be handed over to immigration authorities. They had already issued a detainer for possible deportation.

In my mind I was guilty, because I lied. I wondered if the judge would accept my plea and justify my conviction. Pleading guilty by lying was in fact the most gullible thing I have ever done in my entire life.

Judge Taylor, in the second Judicial District court, accepted this plea of guilty. At that moment, I became a convicted felon and lost my constitutional rights.

On sentencing day, March 27, 1980, the Judge announced a sentence for a maximum of 8 years for both charges. At this time, he did not know the content of the plea agreement. He also didn't know that prior to the plea bargain the fourteen counts of theft were thrown out by Judge James Sullivan. I was shocked at the verdict. What happened to my plea agreement?

Judge Taylor was presented with the arson case and the theft charges. But the theft charges had previously been dismissed and my Public Defender had withdrawn from the case. This left me without legal counsel. The Judge was handed false information. With all these trickery games, my sentence was announced, min 5 years, max 8 years, for both offenses concurrent. I wanted to convince the court, but Judge Taylor would not let it happen.

As I left the courthouse, escorted by police, the media rushed toward me and a crowd had gathered yelling and creating quite a commotion. The police did their best to push them away. A reporter from the Denver Post managed to shove his way through the crowd getting close enough to me to present a question: "Why did you plead guilty?" The police pushed the reporter along, but I was able to yell out, "I was morally responsible for four customers who paid money and did not get their airline tickets nor their refund. I will pay them back when things are settled!"

The following day, March 28, the Denver newspaper read:

Rocky Mountain News - March 28, 1980

INDIAN NATIVE GETS EIGHT YEARS IN TRAVEL SWINDLE

And other local papers said:

JUDGE SEARS INDIAN NATIONAL BILKING DOZENS IN REGION

And:

EX-TRAVEL AGENCY OWNER INDICTED

I was to be transferred to Canyon City State Penitentiary. While I waited for the transfer, the thought of dying in a prison system scared me. My rights seemed non-existent. Being a Hindu, and believing the natural laws laid down in Hinduism, I felt desperate. My mind was frantically trying to figure out what I could do to save my life. "Before an ant dies, God gives it wings to fly to have its freedom for a few seconds." Before all doors were closed for me, I requested a trip to the Ganges River in India to cleanse my sins. "I was a sinner because I have associated with sinners for one year and I rationalize, as a sinner I must bathe in the Ganges to purify my soul."

I wrote my request on a pad of paper on April 1, 1980… my birthday:

> "I would like to go to India for two weeks to wash away my sins in the Ganges River. According to my religion anybody convicted of a crime must wash away his sins within a year. Please allow me to exercise my religious rights."

Again I made headlines in the local newspapers:

INMATE SEEKS BATH - IN GANGES

INMATE REQUESTS TWO-WEEK TRIP TO INDIA

HE WANTS A VACATION FROM PRISON

And:

AID ON WAY FOR HINDU IN QUEST OF HOLY BATH

I handed over the papers to the guard to process it through the proper multiple channels: supervisor, captain, warden, chief sheriff, then to the governor. After two long weeks of waiting, I received a letter from the secretary to the governor of Colorado expressing concern for my meeting my religious rights. The secretary contacted several leaders of the Indian community living in Colorado to find a solution for this problem. Perhaps my deportation had already been decided, as part of the game.

Perhaps it was suggested that a small amount of holy water from the Ganges River mixed with local water would be sufficient for washing away my sins. I sent a letter back saying it was not acceptable. I must immerse myself physically in the Ganges, until then, the purification is not complete. I also needed a priest from a particular temple in India.

The Indian Embassy in Washington was informed to make arrangements for me to travel to India escorted by two US Marshals. But the Indian government said they could not guarantee the safe return of the escorts. Needless to say, many months went by and my request went unresolved.

When I entered Canyon City Penitentiary, a high security prison, all my belongings, including my Green Card, Indian Passport, driver's license, and all my credit cards were sent to my parent's address in Gwalior, India. I now had no proof of my identity, no proof of my legal status in the USA, and no proof as an immigrant, I needed to have these papers.

Since I was not a security risk and not a violent person, I was soon eligible to go to a minimum-security camp called Delta Honor Camp near Grand Junction, Colorado. Here, I would be more comfortable and could do my own cooking. That move probably saved my life. I got to cook my style of vegetarian food.

The store supply manager was a stout, Mexican man who scurried around with a big smile on his face. He managed all the food, clothes, and other necessities needed for running the camp. Once a week he'd drive to Denver to pick up supplies and I'd give him a short list of items that I needed, such as spices, and lentils, and names and addresses of a few Indian grocery stores. Somehow he managed to buy my things along with his required long list.

The kitchen supervisor, a good-natured man, kept me informed when the kitchen was available for me to cook my food. After the one hundred twenty inmates had finished their own meal, I could prepare mine. He provided me with whatever pots and utensils I needed.

He often asked me to eat the inmates' food instead, and I would tell him, "I don't eat anything that used to walk, run, fly, or curl."

"What's wrong with eggs? They don't run or fly!" he proclaimed.

"I just don't eat eggs. Eggs are a transformation of a soul and it's a life after all," I explained.

Most of the inmates and staff made fun of my eating habits, but "inside their hearts," they respected my way of thinking.

When the Counselor General of India, based in San Francisco, visited me, he was given a tour of the facility including the kitchen, and the officials explained my daily routine.

He was satisfied with my situation there and pleased with the way my affairs were handled. He refused to eat lunch at the camp, but I was allowed to make him a cup of *marsala chai.*

Most of the guards eventually wanted to taste my food. In fact, one of my counselors enjoyed my cooking so much, he became a vegetarian!

One thing that bothered me about my current situation was the fact that inmates who were citizens were allowed parole, but because my detainer was held up in Immigration Court, I did not have that privilege.

I could have walked away like several inmates had done, but I tried to abide by the laws of the Colorado Department of Correction.

Sometimes, when a helicopter was sighted flying over the camp, the inmates jokingly would yell out, "Maybe Indira Gandhi sent a helicopter to rescue you!"

The camp turned out to be a source of knowing "real America." The men came from all walks of life. Most were successful businessmen, intellectuals, and hard-working men who had made some minor mistakes. Most would leave the camp, be welcomed back into society, and return to their normal lives.

Many letters came from family, friends, my wife Jane, and from high officials of the Indian Government inquiring about my well-being and wanting to know when I would be released. The Indian Ambassador was required by the Indian Prime Minister to report on my condition and also to inform my family in Gwalior. I wrote letters to my friends and family reassuring them that I was in good health and having a good time cooking, playing football, reading, watching TV, and writing letters. I was also chosen to be the librarian to operate the Camp Library. I wrote many letters to Jane explaining my confusion when I had been, once again, presented with divorce papers.

After being at Delta Honor Camp for several months, I was transported to an Appeals Court in Denver. My sentence, under the Federal rule of criminal procedure, Rule 35, was up for reconsideration. This meant my sentence could be reduced.

I imagined I would walk to the plane like a free man. But, I was not free. A guard greeted me, holding a heavy metal chain with four cuffs attached. It surprised me to think that these shackles were for me. My wrists and ankles were securely locked to make sure I did not run away! I shuffled to a high security car, was driven to the plane, and clamored clumsily up the plane's long staircase.

Again, Judge Taylor was to decide the appeal for my case. Sam Harris drew specific attention to the court, explaining, "My client, Pradeep Parashar, would not have pleaded guilty unless he had been given certain concessions. The plea agreement was totally ignored. I had misplaced the plea agreement which was made on February 7, 1980, and it was unavailable on the day of sentencing. Judge Taylor expected the Deputy District Attorney, Andrew Burke, to respond to Sam Harris, but he forgot to do so.

The game was played well.

Judge Taylor was disgusted, because he wasn't given the correct information.

At that moment he suspended the sentence and ordered me handed over to US Immigration Authorities to satisfy their detainer for possible deportation.

I was transported back to Delta Honor Camp. I waited a month before all the paperwork was completed. When done, an Immigration Agent arrived on an official four-seater plane to transport me back to Denver. I was told to pack my bags and check out.

I anticipated more injustice.

In Denver, I was placed in the Federal Detention Center, situated in the Denver County Jail. After a couple of weeks I was escorted to the Immigration Court.

Before I entered the Court House lobby, a federal investigator wanted to know my legal immigration status. "I am a permanent resident of this country and I am a green card holder." I said. He asked for me to present my green card.

"My green card," I explained, "and other belongings were sent to my parents' home in Gwalior by the Colorado Department of Corrections which left me without legal documents. In any case the Immigration Department's official record will reveal my legal status, if needed."

I appeared in front of an Immigration Judge to respond to a "show cause notice" and be pardoned under Section 212 (C) of the Immigration and Naturalization Act, as a discretionary power provided by the Attorney General of the US. I also submitted my written statement informing the court that, "I have lived in the United States for more than seven years as a lawful permanent resident. I am not a national security threat, as I am married to a US citizen. The deportation will cause extreme hardship for me and my US citizen wife. I have no legal counsel to present my case, and if I'm released from custody on a "personal recognition bond" I could defend my position in an appropriate manner."

The judge denied change of custody, my bail bond was set at $10,000 and volunteer departure from the US was also denied.

A month later, I appeared again for a deportation hearing. The District Director of the Immigration and Naturalization Service presented this case and suggested to the court that the respondent does not deserve a favorable discretion under Section 212 (C) of INA. I argued that the District Director had not been correctly informed by the Denver District attorney's office.

The "show cause notice" is an order issued by the courts asking a defendant to explain in writing why disciplinary action should not be taken. It also gives a defendant a chance to explain his or her behavior in hopes of avoiding disciplinary action. In my case the notice was supported by misleading information. The two Class 3 felony charges had already been dismissed earlier and the final conviction was two Class 4 felonies arising from a single scheme of misconduct, as is recorded by the Denver District Court in Motion 35B. The District Director should have supported the "show cause notice" for probable deportation based on new and correct information. I felt that it would be highly discriminatory if the "law of mercy" were unavailable to me.

Misusing discretionary power is against the law. I considered this to be a systematic discrimination. I felt it was injustice number one.

I was hoping that someone would bail me out and I would be free, but unfortunately no one came to support me, nobody signed the bail bond. Jane had given up on me.

There was a popular Hindi song that kept going through my mind and drove me crazy:

> *"When someone breaks your heart and leaves you in uncomfortable situation, then you come to me, my door is open and will remain open for you. Now, you do not need me, you find many seekers. For now you are an ocean of beauty. As many lotuses as you desire will bloom for you ... When your own image in the mirror starts to scare you ... When youth begins to leave you, then you will come to me, beloved. There is no condition in love, but you have fallen in love. When the stars, started to shine and now extinguished, the light of the spiritual relationship; when you start falling in your own eyes and surrounded in the dark of your own darkness, then you come to me, dear...*

In January of 1981, with great disappointment, I was flown to LA and then boarded the same Pan Am Flight 001 that took Jane and me around the world in eighty days. This time, alone, I would fly home, back to India.

Again, if I could have been given a pardon and my bond

paid and if the US Attorney General in his discretion, had granted me relief, I could have gone back to society and paid my clients back like I promised.

As I boarded the plane, I panicked. I didn't have the document with me which I needed to get into India.

"Where's my travel document?" I yelled.

"It was given to the pilot and he will hand it to the authorities when you arrive in New Delhi," the guard reassured me. I sat on the Pan Am Flight 001 with all my memories. I'm leaving America but not in my heart. I promised myself that I would return to the US to bring the truth to my friends and family. I had a lot of time to think and reminisce about my past: my business, Jane, friends, my future. I was a man caught between two worlds, the East and the West.

I did okay spending sixteen months in Denver County Jail and Delta Honor Camp which was a very nice place to have extra holidays!

The only heavy thing was accepting divorce from Jane to whom I had promised a commitment for life. She called from Martha's Vineyard the day before I left and asked for a divorce. I agreed. I did not want to be a failure to maintain my responsibility, especially for Jane, a super, soft-hearted, intelligent and caring soul whom I would never hurt physically, spiritually, or cause any problem in any way, whatsoever. This is me; me who went undetected from developing the understanding of love. Needless to say, I would always care for her, as there is no such thing as too late, everything has its own time. Sometimes, we expect it at the wrong time. It is our ignorant karma which results in irritation, anxiety or uncertainty in our mind which makes life disturbed and our dreams remain dreams. There would always be some risk. We try to avoid blind risk and prefer only calculated risks. We must be brave, for only the bold can manage it. But, no risk… no thrill, no life.

When the plane landed in New Delhi, I was exhausted, but at the same time, excited to see my family. A new beginning stood before me and I had to be optimistic. I gathered my belongings, exited the plane and headed toward customs. As I walked along, I realized the pilot had never given me my travel document, so I turned around and ran back to the terminal. The plane, continuing to Hong Kong, had already left and the pilot had neglected to hand over my papers to anyone.

After the customs clearance, Indian Immigration officials asked for passport and identity and I didn't have them. Indian authorities needed to verify my identity. I asked if I could make a phone call and I took out a crumpled piece of paper on which I had written down a number that Rakesh had sent me. The telephone number was that of India's Prime Minister, Indira Gandhi. When the security officer saw her name and phone number, he yelled out to the immigration officer, "Let him go home!"

Rakesh greeted me with warmth and compassion as a brother would. It felt comforting to see a familiar friendly face, someone happy to see me. It was a long five-hour train ride back to Gwalior. The streets looked familiar, crowded with people, cars, and cows. Nothing had changed since I had left almost twelve years ago. Rakesh and I talked the entire way home and when we arrived at my mother's house many friends and relatives were there to greet me. It turned into a celebration, filled with stories, questions and tears.

I had originally left India and its ancient ways to seek adventure and establish myself in the West as a businessman in the travel industry. That had been my dream. I took many risks. I learned to be cheeky and conniving in order to survive. But I did not commit the crimes I was convicted of. I have loved and been loved, have served people sincerely and have lived my life to its fullest. The heat, the chaos, the squalor, and the ancient traditions of India still exist, but I now have the strength and fortitude to create a new life, new dreams.

I am okay.
I didn't lose everything.

And when I close my weary eyes, I smile and picture the paper bag and $30,000 safely buried in Golden Gate Park!

EPILOGUE

JANE

My future plans with Pradeep were gone. I didn't know where I belonged. I was confused and depressed. I decided to leave Martha's Vineyard and move back to California where I found an apartment in Berkley and a teaching position in San Francisco. I agonized over re-inventing my life. I filled my time trying to begin again.

In October, 1979, I wrote Pradeep:

> Dear Pradeep,
>
> Haven't heard from you for a while. How are things going? I'm very disappointed in Sam Harris. He said he would call two weeks ago and hasn't yet gotten in touch with me. Today I went into a store called Bombay Bazaar. Had a great time smelling the spices and incense and tasting some Indian food. They had a record playing, the Indian music sounded so familiar and I thought of you.
>
> Pradeep, how much fun it

would have been to stay together. My life still hasn't settled into a routine, but I've got a job and a place to live, my health is good. My mind is somewhat together, and I stay firm on a lot of issues that we had. I think of all I've been through and get a little depressed, but I get over it.

Please, write a sincere letter next time. I don't want to hear about demons and God … I want words from the heart, rational, honest and sincere, about you, about me. Also, if you need anything let me know. I'll be happy to send it to you.

The teachers' strike is over and schools are underway. The other L.D.G (Learning Disabilities Group) teacher has joined me, and we are putting our program together. Got tickets to see Bob Dylan in November. $15 a ticket. It was my birthday present to myself. Ugh, another year older!

Take care and write. Love,

Jane

The middle school was in a rough area of the city and I could not deal with the lack of respect the students had for their school or teachers. In January of 1980, I resigned,

I wanted a job with as little stress as possible which I found in Jack London Square at a gourmet cafe. It was perfect: a small, classy place serving delicious, creative food.

After several months of making quiches and cappuccinos, however, I decided it was time to leave California and move back to the East Coast. A fresh start was needed. I packed my belongings into my VW Bug "hippie mobile" and set off driving north, first to Seattle then to Vancouver, took a right and headed east across Canada. I camped in parks and my only fear was waking up to a bear! There was a tranquility that followed me as I traveled along the back roads. The freedom revitalized me. I didn't know what the future would be, but perhaps my karma would be clearer during this next leg of my life. When I reached Toronto, I headed south and made my way back to Martha's Vineyard.

It felt good to be back on the island. I moved into an apartment in a vintage carriage house in Vineyard Haven and when settled, I invited my elderly landlady for tea. We sat in the cozy, dimly lit kitchen and talked. She shared many stories of her childhood on the Vineyard and of her travels as a young woman. After college, she had had an opportunity to travel to India as a missionary and teach school. I was intrigued and asked her where in India was the school. I hadn't yet mentioned my saga and when she answered, "Gwalior. Have you heard of it?" I stared at her in disbelief. She had taught at the Carmel Convent School, founded by the Carmelite Sisters of St. Teresa. The school opened in 1957 in order to teach English to the common people of India. I proceeded to tell my story … most of it anyway. We had a delightful discussion of our experiences in India, hers in the late 1950's and mine in 1979. What were the chances of my meeting someone on an island in a small town who would have heard of Gwalior, let alone had lived there? Karma?

Soon after I arrived, I met with two friends who were interested in opening a boutique.

It sounded like a good plan to me and I needed a job. The store would feature traditional handwoven and hand-knit items, and as a person who loved to sew, I would design and make clothing using ethnic fabrics. We found an upstairs space for rent in a renovated old house in Edgartown and called our little boutique "Traditions." I kept busy sewing and designing clothes which distracted me somewhat from thoughts of Pradeep and the guilt I felt not being able to help him. But no matter how I tried, he was always on my mind.

Our communication continued while he remained in prison, where he tried desperately to prove himself innocent. Nobody would listen. I could see no future for us, so I called him and asked if he would consent to a divorce. He said yes. I filled out the divorce papers at the Edgartown Town Hall and six months later the divorce was finalized. It cost me $50!

Actually, I knew Pradeep would never receive the divorce papers, therefore he never signed anything. Because, he didn't respond within the six-month time frame, the divorce automatically went through.

Shortly after our phone conversation, he was deported. It was January, 1981.

I wanted to love him, but I didn't understand his way of thinking. Was it because of his smoking hash, or his Indian culture, the religion, the traditions that I did not understand?

Was he guilty or not? Nothing made sense.

What magical source drew us together? Karma? Fate?

Together we created an array of excitement, dreams and adventures, running full speed with sharp turns and wrong directions, spilling over with sporadic love and emotion, not knowing where we would end up. Then it abruptly came to an end.

The memories of our past play over and over again, and I would change the outcome of this story if I could. We have to live with what we choose, accept our successes and our mistakes and need to be prepared for the unexpected.

Pradeep, not being realistic or sensible, led to his own downfall.

I was naive, idealistic, a romantic, and also not realistic.

In 1979 we were searching for something new in our lives, needing to enhance our current situations, and desired to challenge the unknown.

Each of us received a life's lesson on trust and expectations. We met by chance, engulfed by desire and pulled apart by bad luck or "ignorant karma."

We stumbled as we tried to understand each other's traditions and cultures and struggled to remain the individuals we were meant to be.

I wanted to write this story with Pradeep to find the truth concerning the robbery, the fire, and to determine if Pradeep was guilty or not? Does it matter? At this time, not really.

Sometimes we are left with questions and are given no answers. Perhaps that's not so bad. I heard a recording while passing through the Denver Art Museum once where an abstract artist said, "What people don't understand evokes discussion. Discussion keeps people interacting with each other. Continuing to search for answers, creates more questions and keeps the mind alive."

A few years after Pradeep was deported, I flew back to San Francisco and enrolled in the San Francisco School of Massage. In 1985 I returned to Massachusetts and settled in Falmouth where I opened the Healing Arts Center for alternative health. In 1989 I married Jim Doutt. He loved the outdoors and had traveled to many countries with his job at Woods Hole Oceanographic Institution in Woods Hole, Massachusetts. We had two children and with them continued our travel adventures: exploring Italy's Appenine Mountains, hiking the Hardenavenga in Norway and sailing to and around the Bahamas for seven months on our 37-foot Prout Catamaran, "Iso Kala."

As a family and independently, we continue to explore our world and its people with gratitude and respect.

~

Cape Cod, 2019

The egret settles itself down into the water, the osprey circles the sky, and the grackles fly from tree to tree making a racket of gossip amongst their neighborhood.

I sit on the porch sipping my morning coffee and gaze out over the marsh. The water sparkles and the breeze is cool.

EPILOGUE

Pradeep

After I pleaded guilty on February 8, 1980 and served 246 days in prison, the immigration court found me deportable as charged, denied my bail request, and ordered me deported to India. On January 15, 1981, I returned home.

On my arrival, my mother told me she had begun planning my wedding and that she had arranged for me to meet with several eligible Hindu women. I agreed to marry a highly-educated Indian woman, and on June 15, 1981 a big wedding celebration was held in Gwalior. I was amazed at how many people attended the wedding. Mrs. Gandhi, the Prime Minister, was expected at the dinner party, but was unable to make it, so a few of her envoys showed up.

I worked for the Indian Tourist Industry for ten years and my wife and I had three children. Working for the government was a good job, but I wanted to be my own boss and work for myself. In 1991, I returned to the U.S. I flew to San Francisco and retrieved my money from Golden Gate Park – yes, it was still there!

From that moment, I had enough money to open World Ways Travel on Market Street, rent an apartment and buy a car. I stayed in the States for five years, proving myself to be a respected and responsible businessman and able to provide for my family.

I found, however, the best place to go was home. But, for me, it was questionable, as my heart was in the West, and physically I lived in the East.

I like India not because I am born here, but India answers many of my questions like: "Who am I?" India offers me the things I need; peace and happiness, modes of karma, getting good results, and my freedom to be with God. My mother had "heard" I had married an American woman, but I avoided talk on that subject, about my past experience in the West. This made it uncomplicated.

Everyone has their own story. Ours is just one more. Whether you are living in the present or in the past, these stories are based on certain conditions. An example of a condition is Lord Brahma's story from the Hindu holy book, *Ramayan*.

It is a story of Lord Brahma and his wife Sita. Their marriage relationship was based on a specific condition or requirement: Sita's father, King Janack, said, "Whoever can break the arrow will be the appropriate person to marry my daughter, Sita." Several men tried to break the arrow but only Brahma succeeded.

The relationship between me and Jane also had specific conditions. As a teacher in San Francisco, Jane's dream was to travel to different countries and gain a better understanding of the world. As a travel agent living in Denver, I wanted to marry someone who would travel and walk with me and share my lifestyle. The two of us meeting, with these two purposes in mind, was karma itself.

In our lifetime unexpected events occur and we have choices and need to make decisions. Some choices lead us down a good path and others down a more turbulent path. We then need to take responsibility for the decisions we make. Dilemma always strengthens our character and promotes realization, perhaps, enlightenment. Jane and I had two different lives, each of us from two different cultures and destined to go two separate ways.

The raindrops from the sky,
If it is caught in hands
it is pure enough for drinking

If it falls in the gutter,
it's value drops so much
that it can't be used
even for washing feet

If it falls on hot surface
it perishes

If it falls on Lotus Leaf,
it shines like a pearl

And finally, if it falls on
oyster, it becomes a pearl

The drop is the same, but it's
existence and worth depend
upon with whom it
associates

Swami Vivekananda

Jane and Pradeep at their wedding,
Gardner, Massachusetts, March 10, 1979

AND JUST ONE MORE THING ...

RECIPES FOR YAMUNA'S GUESTS

MATAR PANEER CURRY

Tomatoes - 250 gms (one cup)
Paneer cubes (a type of cheese) - 250 gms (one cup)
Matar (green peas) - 250 gms (one cup)
Ghee (purified butter / oil)

The first thing my mother Yamuna did was to make a curry paste with fresh ginger, chili powder, coriander, raw turmeric, and a little salt, grinding them together with a little water to make the thick paste. She washed and cut the tomatoes into small pieces. Two cups of water were boiled on top of a kerosene burner. Tomatoes were placed into a pot and boiled for 10-15 minutes. On another stove she deep-fried the *paneer* cubes. After the skins were removed from the tomatoes, she ground them. In *kadai*, a deep frying pan, she added cooking oil. When it became hot, she added 1/2 teaspoon cumin seed for 2-3 seconds, then added the paste along with tomatoes and green peas, smashing the mixture together. The mixture cooked on a low flame until the oil oozed. After 10-12 minutes, she added the fried *paneer* cubes and let simmer for 5-7 minutes. On top of the dish she spread fresh coriander for garnishing.

My mother cooked very simple food, even for special guests. A typical menu included: potato curry, vegetable *pulao, raita* and/or *puris* or *chole masala, dal,* etc. She made the effort to make *roti/puri* because the dish absolutely called for it.

She didn't do anything extraordinary, like serving food on gold plates, just with love and affection for the person she was cooking for, husband, son, daughter, friends, etc.

After our meal together with Carol and Chris, Carol said to my mother, "Mami, you cooked such simple food, but I could feel your love when I ate it. Thank you. Namaste." My father translated.

Every meal included *dal.*

Yamuna used to say, "Nothing beats a *dal* made with love."

GHEE - Purified Butter

I'd make *ghee*, purified butter, by heating two pounds of butter in a deep pot and heating it on an extremely low flame until the fat and the clear part of the butter separated naturally. Then I'd filter it. The clear portion is *ghee* and the remaining portion is fat and waste. Of course, the clear part is what is used.

DAL - Lentil Soup

Many people I met outside of India had very little understanding of vegetarianism. Indian families who refrain from meat carry out this tradition throughout generations.

Vimal, my older brother, convinced me of a reliable and scientific theory of healthy vegetarian food to be consumed in our daily life. According to him," nature has created two types of grain," male and female and they each have their own quality. When the skin is peeled off the grain and splits, such as in *Moong Dal/Yellow Split Gram, Arthar/Pigeon Pea, Masoor Dal/Red Lentil*, the lentils are recognized as male grains and are considered a "cold food," – "*Dhuli.*" The whole lentil that remains a single piece, such as wheat, rice and corn, are female and are considered "hot food," – "*Sabut.*"

Our body temperature is roughly 97 to 98 F. If our body consumes only cold food or only hot food, the food processing machine within our body does not function properly as usual. As a result, a bad stomach could occur. Then we frequently end up in the toilet!

Vimal explained, in order to maintain body temperature constant, we must consume approximately 70% hot food and 30% cold food. With this formula one can avoid stomach disturbances and maintain proper health.

Our family often cooked *moong dal* because it is low in carbohydrates and is a good source of protein. It is a complete package, including essential vitamins such as Vitamin C, K and minerals like iron, potassium, magnesium, copper and zinc. To top it off, *dal* is low in calories and a high source of fibre and antioxidants.

Pradeep's *Dal* Recipe

Wash 1/2 cup lentils several times in a pot with running water, drain. Put lentils into a pressure cooker and add enough water to cover 2" above lentils. Add 1/4 tsp turmeric powder (*Haldi*) and 1/4 tsp salt (*Namak*). I almost always add slit green chilies. Place the pressure cooker over high heat until it boils, then turn burner down to low heat for 15min or until the whistle blows twice. Let it sit off burner for 5 to 7 minutes.

In another pan, heat oil or *ghee*, add the *jeera* (cumin), tomatoes and garlic cloves, saute on a high flame till the tomatoes are soft and pulpy, then I add the boiled dal into this with a little water and boil well for 3 to 4 minutes. Add *marsala* to the *dal* and garnish with fresh green coriander. I like to squeeze a little lemon juice to the *dal* to make it tastier. This recipe will make enough for 3 to 4 people. I usually cook for myself, so the leftovers go into the refrigerator and can be reheated the next day.

Dal is always good to eat with steamed rice and *roti* (flat bread), but pita bread or tortillas are good substitutes.

~

Eat well and stay healthy.

Namaste

About Jane

Jane Parhiala has been a Special Education Teacher, a Massage Therapist and owner of an alternative health center. Since her retirement in 2012, she has devoted her time to writing and weaving. Her weavings have been exhibited in many local art galleries and she is a member of the National League of American Pen Women, Cape Cod Branch. Jane continues to seek adventure and finds time to travel to different parts of the world as well as to her cabin in Vermont. She lives in Falmouth, Massachusetts with her husband.

About Pradeep

Pradeep Parashar has worked in the travel industry in India and the United States for over four decades. He opened Alien Travel Service and World Ways Travel Co. in Chicago, IL in 1972 and moved the business to Denver in 1976. When he returned to India in 1981, he worked for the Indian Government in the Tourism Industry and eventually, established his own travel business. He currently manages two hotels near the Taj Mahal in Agra. He enjoys his time meeting and serving international travelers. He travels frequently between Agra and Gwalior where his family lives.

Made in the USA
Middletown, DE
19 June 2021